ULTRA DISTANCE RUNNING WORLD RECORD BREAKERS!

ULTRA DISTANCE RUNNING

WORLD RECORD BREAKERS!

Chris O'Carroll

Matador
9 Priory Business Park,
Wistow Road, Kibworth Beauchamp,
Leicestershire, LE8 0RX
Tel: 0116 279 2299
Email: books@troubador.co.uk
Web: www.troubador.co.uk/matador
Twitter: @matadorbooks

ISBN 978 183859 128 1

British Library Cataloguing in Publication Data.
A catalogue record for this book is available from the British Library.

Printed and bound by CPI Group (UK) Ltd, Croydon, CR0 4YY
Typeset in 11pt Aldine401 BT by Troubador Publishing Ltd, Leicester, UK

Matador is an imprint of Troubador Publishing Ltd

FSC MIX
Paper from
responsible sources
FSC® C013604
www.fsc.org

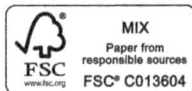

How did four 'Joe Average' club runners
turn into four ultra distance legends!

On road and athletic tracks,
50km to 384km across UK and into Europe!

The inside story of how we did it!

From 1979 to 1983

Gloucester AC Ultra Distance Squad rewrote the record books
racing all over Europe

With many ecstatic highlights, huge disappointments, bad race
organisers and people cheating along the way!

CONTENTS

FOREWORD

Arthur Daley
Gloucester Athletic Club

Chris asked me to write this foreword some time ago. He surprised me by telling me his account of the exploits of the Gloucester Athletic Club ultra-distance runners of the 80s was ready for publication. In doing this he replicated the energy and commitment shown not only by himself and Martin Daykin, Dave Dowdle and Ken Leyshon as they trained and raced over the roads and tracks of Gloucestershire.

This was a time when marathon running was becoming popular, but running, let alone racing, over distances longer than a marathon was the realm of specialists who were perhaps a little different mentally to everybody else! The training as Chris details involved running up to a marathon a day, although sometimes in two sessions; it requires both physical and mental strength.

I was involved in many ways; my first memory is of the influential Malcolm Campbell running vest-less in the first 100-mile race from Tirley, Gloucestershire as I helped with decathletes Paul and Phillip Karlson on a drink station. Gloucester AC was a small club then, and all the sections helped, even if they didn't understand the attraction of running such long distances.

There were times I was more involved. We recruited volunteers and had a great team from Bourton Road Runners for the now famous 24-hour race where Dave Dowdle set a new world track record, Martin Daykin narrowly missing one and innumerable national records set. Two memories from that event stand out: searching for straw to put beneath the feet of the lap scorers as they were in the wettest area outside the track and commentating for the final hour of Dowdle's epic race. Every step is a world record. This was an exciting and unique time: Daykin returning from victory in a French village ultra-race with a side of beef as the prize, taking the team prize in the first Bristol Marathon – I was in my only marathon, fourth man, to score 25 minutes behind the third Gloucester man and they wondered if I'd got lost but still we won the team prize – and remembering the crowds lining both sides of the track for Dowdle's final hour in his world-beating race.

How did it all begin?

By the late 1970s, many runners had run in races up to marathon distances. Few athletes had run longer distances; those athletes that ran further than marathons were considered eccentric or weird!

The four athletes in this story were your joe average club runners competing in athletics on the track and in cross-country, road and trail races, but in 1979 something happened!

Ken Leyshon and Martin Daykin had recently run a marathon race. Ken remarked, "I bet I can run further than you."

Jokingly, Martin said, "You're on."

They looked for a race longer than a marathon and found one in Scotland: The Two Bridges Race. Both ran in it and completed it, with Martin running a blinder, finishing 4th, and Ken finishing a respectable 35th position.

When back in Gloucester, their run had created a lot of interest, in particular for one member, a certain Dave Dowdle. Ken mentioned we might have been among the team prizewinners if we had had another runner. Dave promptly said, "Count me in your next race."

So there were now three in search of their next race and they found it! The 54-mile London to Brighton road race. At the time, this was the longest road running race in England.

They ran the race and couldn't believe it! Gloucester team won it!

More about both races later in the book.

This created even more interest in the club back in Gloucester. Chris O'Carroll had also decided to join them. So now there were four! The Glos Ultra-Distance Squad was up and ready to race in 1979.

PROFILES

Gloucester AC Ultra Squad

Dave Dowdle

Born in Gloucestershire 7/11/1954

Joined Gloucester AC in 1970.

Height 5ft 4" tall

Weight 10st 2lbs

25 years old youngest in the squad.

Worked for an electrical company in Gloucester. Competed in club events, junior and senior in track, cross-country and road races.

Dave liked his pint of Guinness and foodwise, had a colossal appetite consuming 8,000 to 10,000 calories a day

Drank Coke, fruit juices, water and energy drinks

10-mile PB 53mins 10secs.

PB Marathon 2hrs 34mins 43secs.

Ran longer distances with Ken and Martin in 1979.

Dave could do up to (believe me) a thousand press ups non stop!

Dave's hobbies were eating, drinking, training...not much time for anything else.

Chris O'Carroll

Born in Southampton 3/12/1943

Joined Gloucester AC in late 1970s

Height 5ft 10"

Weight 11st 5lbs

Oldest man in the squad at 37 years of age

Previous clubs: Army, combined services,
Nottingham AC, Tipton Harriers, represented
Midlands 3AAAs in track and cross-country

Worked for Wall's Ice cream before going into
sport retail and travel business, Gloucester
Sports

Married with three children

Started Ultra-Distance races with Gloucester AC
in 1981

Diet: mainly fruit and veg, rice, pasta. Vast amount
of calories consumed – 8,000+ – when in
training for longer distance races

Drank varied drinks, including energy drinks, tea,
coffee and water

10-mile PB 49mins 10secs. 30km 1hr 36mins.
Marathon 2hrs 22mins

Ken Leyshon

Born in Cheltenham 7/1/1949

Height 5ft 8"

Weight 10stone 5lbs

Married with four children, and brother Greg who encouraged Ken to enter his first marathon in 1978 with a time of 2hrs 42mins 30secs

Started doing ultras in 1979 at 30 years of age. Worked mainly in the furniture removal business

When training hard, diet included lots of fruit and veg, plus steak and fish, but definitely liked a Chinese meal on weekends

Drank tea or coffee, but drank energy drinks, fruit-based drinks and water when running. Liked a pint or two, especially after a hard race

10-mile PB 59mins

Leisure time and hobbies: collecting vinyl classic pop singles from the 60s, 70s, 80s. Quite a collection to this day!

Martin Daykin

Born in Manchester 14/06/1947

Height 6ft 2"

Weight 12stone 4lbs

Moved to Gloucester in 1970 (ex-rugby player who liked a cigarette or two)

Worked in Gloucester City as a quantity surveyor. Married to Liz Daykin

Like Ken, started running ultra distances when he was 32 years of age

Competed at club level in cross-country and road races, until switching to longer distances with Ken in 1979 (p.s. packed up the smoking)

Martin's hobbies and leisure time included a love of natural history, and classic motor cars, owning a Lancia among others over the years. Also loved his music

Enjoyed all kinds of foods, ate up to 8000 cals+ when in training

Drank a mixture of Coke, orange squash, water, but known to drink a beer or two during a race towards the end!

Also spoke French, German, Spanish and Czech, which was quite handy when racing abroad

PBs ASAT 1979, marathon 2hrs 35mins 00secs

54 miles London to Brighton 5hrs 45mins 06secs

P R E F A C E

So there you have it, a brief profile of Gloucester Ultra-Distance Squad, proving that there is no such thing as an ideal shape for ultra-distance runners.

They come in all shapes and sizes, with different likes and hobbies, but what they do have in common is a love of running; whether it's on the roads, trails or athletic tracks, they will compete and train, in all weathers.

A lot of our training was mostly on hilly terrains (as you will see later on in the book). From 1979 to 1983, see how the Glos Squad gradually improved into one of the strongest ultra-distance running squads in the world!

Lots of mishaps, bitter disappointments and unforgettable moments. Even dealing with cheating and bad race organisation. It was like we had served an apprenticeship, as we finally brought some of the world's best ultra-distance   runners to Gloucester City's cinder track and not only beat them, but set various world and national records along the way! Also mentioned in the book are the ladies who competed with us on some of our journeys; fellow kindred spirits, who also pioneered their way in setting world and national records in ladies' ultra-distance running.

We will also not forget to mention the wonderful backing we had from everyone in Gloucester and further afield, who went on this journey with us. Families, fellow athletes, various running club officials, marshals, RRC of Great Britain, volunteer helpers and other sponsors too. (Although I do think most came along to see because they thought we were all mad.)

I would also like to quickly mention Stan Dalby, Dave Price, Les Davis, Joanne Davis, John Conlon, Brian Healy and Neil Jones, who competed in some of our ultra races as well!

So without further ado, I really hope this book will inspire you on your own journey, whatever distances you run!

Just do it and enjoy it!

THE MAIN ITINERARY

1979 to 1983

Date	Race	Country	Distance/Hrs
30/09/1979	London to Brighton Road Race	UK	54 miles
06/04/1980	Niort	France	50km
23/08/1980	Two Bridges Race Rosyth	Scotland	36 miles+
11/04/1981	100 mile road race Gloucestershire	UK	100 miles
08/1981	Two Bridges Race Rosyth	Scotland	36 miles+
24-25/10/1981	Brest to Rennes 6 man relay race	France	267km
22-23/05/1982	24hour Track Race Gloucester	UK	24 Hour
06/06/1982	100km Road Race to Paris	France	100km
28/08/1982	Two Bridges Race Rosyth	Scotland	36 miles +
11/09/1982	100km Winston European Road Race Championships	Holland	100km
02/04/1983	24 hour 4x1mile Relay Chilternham	UK	24 Hour Relay
13-14/05/1983	48 hour Track Race Gloucester	UK	48 Hour

R A C E 1

In September 1979, a three-man Glos AC Team entered the longest road race in the UK, 54 miles+, the 29th running of the London to Brighton road race, Sunday, 30th September, 1979.

Little did Martin Daykin, Dave Dowdle and Ken Leyshon know that they were beginning a journey they would never forget!

This race ended with lots of firsts for the team. The race itself was won first time by Allan Kirk from the USA, in a time of 5hrs 32mins and 37secs.

Martin ran an outstanding race to finish 2nd in a time of 5hrs 45mins and 06secs.

Ken finished 20th in a time of 6hrs 18mins 31secs, and 21st was Dave with a time of 6hrs, 19mins and 46secs.

1st Team Gloucester A.C.	2nd Team Millrose AA New York USA
Martin J Daykin 1	J Erskine 5
Ken A Leyshon 6	D Obelkevich 9
Dave M Dowdle 7	H W Stern 14
14 points	28 points

When the results sheets were produced, Gloucester AC nearly swept the board.

2nd Martin Daykin – Memento Plaque – Gloucester AC Team Winners – 'Len Hurst' Belt – Gloucester AC

This was the most prestigious race, with an entry from five continents taking part. So Gloucester Ultra-Distance Squad was up and running (with three members to date).

The Gloucester AC team who won the London to Brighton road race photographed with their president, Coun. John Robins, at Black Bridge, the club's headquarters. Left to right : Ken Leyshon (20th), Martin Daykin (2nd), and Dave Dowdle (21st).

3

R A C E 2

After Glos Ultra-Distance Squad's great results in the London to Brighton Race, the three of them, Dave, Ken and Martin, were invited abroad to **The 50km Baratange-International – Niort, 6th April 1980.**

The Gloucester team's first race abroad… I'll hand you over to Martin who wrote this article about their whole experience that weekend!

VAINQUEUR

Martin DAYKIN
GLOUSCESTER A.C.

– ANGLETERRE–
2H 58'47"

DEUXIEME

Bernard GAUDIN
SPIRIDON POITOU CHARENTES

– FRANCE –
3H 00'50"

6ème 50 KM INTERNATIONAL
Michel BARATANGE
DIMANCHE 6 AVRIL 1980
NIORT (France)
PARTICIPANTS
GRAND FOND PEDESTRE A STYLE LIBRE
OUVERT A TOUS ET TOUTES
DANS L'ESPRIT DES 100 Km DE MILLAU
DEPART 9 h . PLACE DE LA BRECHE
record de l'épreuve: WOODWARD cavin 2h57 (ANGLETERRE)
organisé par: LE SCULPTURAL CLUB NIORTAIS
et le: SPIRIDON CLUB
POITOU CHARENTES
78, Rue de BESSAC - 79000 NIORT
Tel. 24 - 34 - 79
25 km
Charchenais
STE-NEOMAYE
NIORT
Souché
Chavagné
La Chesnaye
Les Fontenelles
La Rivière
Champclairot
Départ
Arrivée
50 km
A BIENTOT ET TOUS AU RENDEZ-VOUS !

PALMARES
DIMANCHE
6 AVRIL
1980
NIORT
50 KM
Michel
BARATANGE

THE SIXTH INTERNATIONAL BARATANGE 50KM TROPHY RACE, NIORT, 1980

Martin Daykin

Having tasted the atmosphere of running abroad but once before, I was delighted

to receive an invitation to compete in this race in France on 6th April, and to savour once again the tremendous enthusiasm of continental races.

Gloucester AC teammates Ken Leyshon and Dave Dowdle were equally delighted to complete the three-man team.

We used the Duchy Marathon as a depletion run, but it was over our third pint afterwards that we remembered that carbohydrates were supposed to be taboo until Thursday. To make amends, we kept the mileage high all through the week. My wife and brother Tony accompanied us to France. We had an inauspicious start, as just after the ferry, we found that the French customs were having a go-slow.

We eventually arrived at Niort, between Nantes and Bordeaux, at 2 am. Since Ken, Dave and I knew our host, Michel Rouille, was not only an accomplished athlete but also the French weight-lifting champion of squats, we goaded Tony into waking him up. Seeing that Michel was delighted to see us, despite the hour, we emerged from our hiding place and were warmly welcomed by him and his charming wife, Michelle.

At breakfast next morning, we learnt that Don Ritchie had not yet arrived. Press and TV had been giving a big build-up, and Don's picture appeared on many posters around the town.

We tried to put people at rest by suggesting that he would arrive close to the start of the race by train, as Malcolm Campbell frequently does. They still looked worried.

Typical of French hospitality, our wish to know something about the course instantly translated into action. An eager chauffeur was summoned, and we were slowly shown around the route.

We ran about 8 miles around the midway point, to get the feel of things. Upon our return to the race headquarters, the organisers were obviously very pleased about something... Don had arrived! Apparently he had been directed to the ferry to Ostend by mistake and had had a lengthy journey through Belgium and France. Local hero, Bernard Gaudin, was less delighted. He planned to win this one, no matter who turned up. He seemed to be still smarting from the 10-minute trouncing in last year's race behind Cavin Woodward.

"No more sleep," came the call at 5.30 am. Our host seemed intent on an early appearance and we staggered down to breakfast to find Don already up, and taking every available container with his on-the-run drinks. In reality, it was 7.30 am. The commencement of French energy-saving time the evening before meant putting our watches on an hour, and not back, as we had done.

We were driven to the start in the town square, and we noted the British runners who were idly watching the world go by.

In contrast, the French runners were busy running on the spot, doing violent P.T. exercises, or in Bernard's case, doing full sprint starts time and time again.

The start was more by general consent than by given order, and the British runners were caught by surprise somewhat. My plan was to watch Don and hope that he would pull me along to a good time. Accordingly, I stuck to his side like a leech as he moved up the field, past Bernard who surprisingly was not latching on to us, and up to the leader, Yves Seigneuric of Paris. The three of us gradually moved away from the rest of the field at about 5.40 pace.

At about 10km, Yves shook things up. He obviously wanted to fly the flag in front of his countrymen, especially the large crowd around the first feeding station. I matched strides with him until he relaxed the pace again. An identical tactic a short distance further on was treated the same way, except that on glancing over my shoulder, I noted that Yves had slowed dramatically and that Don was some way in arrears. Panic! It had been nearly fifteen years since I had been in front of a race, and there were still 40km to go. Gripped by a long dormant feeling of euphoria, I kept the pace fast, accelerating like a raw novice for about 10km.

Echoing footsteps at about 20km convinced me that Don was shadowing me. A quick look revealed it was someone without a number. Tony and Liz drew alongside in the car and explained that my 'rival' had, in fact, just emerged from his gate and was revelling in the shouts from the crowd. Thankfully, he desisted after a short while.

Approaching the halfway stage, I decided to treat whoever was second to a bit of play-acting. I picked up the pace again and started back the way I had come, noting that the time was about 1 hour 28 minutes. A little over a minute later, Bernard came into view, labouring up a steep hill, which I was now descending. Holding my breath and grinning like a Cheshire cat, I uttered a few pleasantries in French; not a flicker from Bernard. Yves and Don gave words of encouragement as we passed, and I noted that Dave and Ken in joint 11th place were looking comfortable. Both looked startled to see me and gave strong vocal support. Several runners actually stopped to applaud as our paths crossed; such was the level of sportsmanship.

Tony looked worried, as nearing the marathon mark, I started to pay for my earlier pace and he told me that Bernard had reduced my lead to around a minute. I had noticed for some time that the myriad of cyclists around the runners had occasionally taken to going in front, stopping and casually looking at their watches as I passed. They were obviously letting Bernard know.

Since the earlier ploy of appearing fresh hadn't convinced Bernard that it was pointless trying to catch me, I decided to lift the pace again, hoping that word would get back to him that it appeared that I had plenty left. It worked! Tony looked optimistic again; the lead widened, despite the fact that I had restarted my labouring stride pattern again.

Approaching the finish, the lead car suddenly bristled with heads shouting, "Three hours, three hours." Looking at my watch, it seemed possible I could do this and I made one last effort. Thinking I had beaten this time by about half a minute, I found it was nearer 75 seconds. The missing three quarters of a minute had puzzled me all along. This was due to the 'start' being 200 metres from the start proper, just outside the town square. Bernard breezed in some 2 minutes later and sportingly shook hands. I was not pleased later on when I read his comments in the paper that whereas he had to work for a living, I was a 'professional'.

It seemed beyond his belief that 140 miles a week could be done with a full-time job. He should see some Leamington AC training diaries!

A short while later, Don arrived, obviously weary from his travelling the previous day. In 4th place, the likeable Frenchman, Yves Seigneuric, was for once not smiling. He made a beeline for Bernard, and from the furious dialogue which ensued, it appeared that Yves was unhappy about the way that Bernard's cycling friends had shielded him from the wind.

It wasn't long, however, before peace was restored.

Dave Dowdle arrived in an inspired 8th position, his second half had enabled him to pick up places. With Ken Leyshon fighting his way to a very game 21st place, Gloucester AC won the team prize!

The presentation ceremony was an embarrassment to the three of us. We had been given hospitality normally reserved for film stars and here we were carrying off a large proportion of their astonishing array of awards. It was quite overwhelming. The evening was rounded off in a Chinese restaurant with our hosts and the other British runners.

It was with genuine sadness that we left Niort next morning. These wonderful people even insisted in filling what little space remained in the boot of our car with a selection of local wines and Champagne. We learnt that on the 10th anniversary of this race in 1984, all the previous winners, as well as the ageless Alain Mimoun, will be invited to compete again; roll on 1984.

I	M. Daykin	Gloucester A.C.	2HR 58MINS 47SECS
2	G. Gaudon		3HRS 50SECS
3	D. Ritchie	Aberdeen A.A.C.	3HR 5MINS 44SECS
4	Y. Seigneuric		3HRS 14MINS 20SECS
5	Meakeo		3HRS 14MINS 37SECS
6	Broton		3HRS 14MINS 40SECS
8	D. Dowdle	Gloucester A.C.	3HRS 17MINS 28SECS
21	K. Leyshon	Gloucester A.C.	3HRS 38MINS 28SECS

Another great result for Gloucester AC Ultra-Distance Team Squad! With this only being our second (three-man squad) race, could this become a habit?

R A C E 3

(As a threeman team)
Two Bridges, Rosyth, Scotland 36 miles+
23 August 1980

The Two Bridges Race 36 miles+ is an ideal distance for ultra-distance runners to move up from the marathon distance.

Gloucester AC third Ultra-Distance Race, as a three-man squad

The thirteenth running of the Two Bridges Race 36miles+ in Rosyth, Scotland 23 August 1980

Our team: Martin Daykin
               Dave Dowdle
               Ken Leyshon

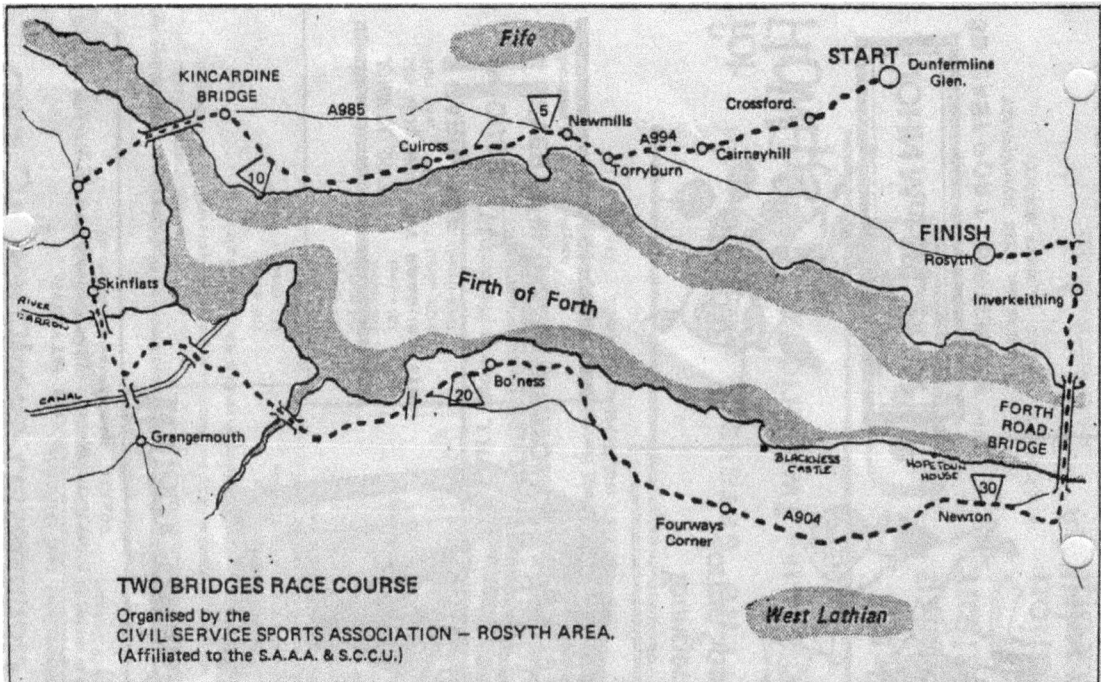

TWO BRIDGES RACE COURSE
Organised by the
CIVIL SERVICE SPORTS ASSOCIATION — ROSYTH AREA.
(Affiliated to the S.A.A.A. & S.C.C.U.)

Martin had an outstanding run, finishing 3rd in a time of 3hrs 34mins 07secs
Dave, improving all the time, was 6th in a time of 3hrs 42mins 05secs
Ken, ever-dependable, finished 39th in a time of 4hrs 30mins 07secs

TEAM TOTAL: 48 points

Finishing 2nd team to Tipton Harriers AC; quite an honour to finish 2nd to Tipton, who were legends in the 1980s and national champions at road and cross-country races and relays.

But watch out, Tipton! We're after you on the Ultra-Distance front!

Another good result for Gloucester AC, but our next race would be our first race as a four-man squad! In a 100-mile road race, in our own backyard in Gloucestershire!

By now, Chris O'Carroll had decided to join the Ultra Glos Squad. So now there was a four-man squad up and running!

RACE 4

(With a four-man Glos AC Squad)
Gloucestershire, England, 100-Mile Road Race
11 April 1981

A race we would never forget!

Our first race as a four-man squad, with Chris O'Carroll having joined the Gloucester Ultra Squad now. He was thinking of having a go at the ultra distances while helping Martin to realise one of his own ambitions: to attack Don Ritchie's 100-mile road world best of 11hrs 51mins 12secs, set in Central Park, New York 1979. Martin devised a flatish course near Tewksbury 10 x 10 mile loops, at Forthampton, a 100-mile road race, in our own backyard! Sounds crazy!

We must have been mad! So with the club's backing, Martin proceeded to formulate and organise this iconic 100-mile road race.

Back to some serious training for this one!

Here's the story I wrote about the whole event back in 1981.

I hope you enjoy reading it; how we prepared, trained for it and carried it out.

GLOUCESTER 100-MILE ROAD RACE, 11 APRIL 1981

The inside story of a race which turned into a classic and completely rewrote the world all-time best ranking lists

It all started back in December 1980. Four of Gloucester Athletic Club's runners were discussing future road races for 1981: Martin Daykin, 33 years old, Chris O'Carroll, 37 years old, Ken Leyshon, 32 years old and Dave Dowdle, 26 years old.

They were tossing around the idea of competing in a 100-mile road race, just to see if they could do it. It was quickly discovered that there were no 100-mile fixtures anywhere in the UK, or even Europe. The English, being an inventive breed, soon found a solution to the problem. Martin remarked rather casually, "Just have to promote the race ourselves!" This crazy idea slowly sunk into the others.

"Yeah, why not?" said Ken, Chris and Dave, nodding in agreement. So began a whole series of events which were to create road-running history and add a bit more folklore to future legends.

The Gloucester Athletic Club and committee (rather surprisingly) quickly fully supported the idea and were to back us all the way. Nobody had any experience of either running a 100-mile race or organising one! What the hell! Who cared? The mountain was there to climb and we were determined to climb it. We were on our way!

Top of the priorities was a suitable course. Poring over the maps, going over the terrain in cars, even running over various courses, suddenly as if guided from above,

there it was: a rather flat 10-mile loop; at one end of it, a big hotel with outbuildings. Two problems solved at once: A. the course and B. changing accommodation.

We approached the hotel proprietor and outlined our whole idea to him. He thought we were all nuts but said, "Okay, you can have the run of the place." The course was quickly surveyed, down to the last inch. The start and finish of each 10-mile loop would be at the hotel itself, ideal, 10x10 mile laps. A date was fixed for the race, 11 April 1981; more daylight and warmer weather then. The race was quickly advertised in Europe and the UK. Astonished to receive fifty-one entries from all over the UK, three from W. Germany. While all this feverish activity was going on, the four Gloucester runners were getting down to the serious business of training. Sixteen weeks' preparation before the race.

Martin, 6'1 1/2" tall, 168 lbs, quickly built up to 140 miles per week. The mileage was held for ten weeks up to the end of March, am 14 miles, pm 8-14 miles. Long runs on Sundays, 4hrs or more.

Dave, 5'5" tall, 144 lbs, built up to 190 miles per week (one week 194!). This he also held for ten weeks to the end of March, am 10 miles, pm 15-20 miles, long runs on Sundays.

Chris, 5'10" tall, 158 lbs and Ken, 5'9" tall, 154 lbs, averaged 120 miles per week, am 5-10 miles, pm 10-15 miles, long runs on Sundays.

OFFICIALS

Referee	:	Mr. R. Freeman
Timekeepers	:	D. Turner
	:	A. Birt
	:	R. Hussey
	:	A. Milroy
Judges	:	M. Price
	:	R. Phillips
	:	K. Mock
Clerk of Course & *Race Secretary*	:	T. Haines
Chief Marshal	:	V. Daykin
Marshals	:	Members of Gloucester Athletic Club

52 ENTERED   ENTRIES FOR 100m   30 STARTED

1	A. HAMACHER	Spiridon Frankfurt (West Germany)
2	H. GARLICK	Wiesbaden (West Germany)
3	G. WERNER ✗	Banberg (West Germany)
4	H. FEDERHEN	Viersen (West Germany)
5	D. HAYWARD	Bristol A.C.
6	D. COFFEY	Cambridge H. (Vet.)
7	T. MOLLETT	" "
8	K. SHAW	" " (Vet.)
9	F. THOMASON	" "
10	M.B. SHIELS	Chelmsford A.C.
11	F. THOMAS	" "
12	S. BROWN	Cheltenham & County H.
14	K. BUCKLE	" " "
15	S. COLVIN	" " "
16	B. HEAFORD	" " "
17	B. IDDON	Chorley A.C.
18	V. PHILLIPS	City of Plymouth A.C.
19	R. SOUL	" " "
20	D. TIPLADY	" " "
21	J. TEESDALE	Durham City H. (Vet.)
22	A. THACKER	East Hull H.
23	J. TOWERS	" " "
24	J. WEBB-POWER	Edinburgh A.C.
25	M. PICKARD	Epsom & Ewell A.C.
26	D. TURNER	" " "
27	B. SLADE	Exeter H.
28	P. HART	Leamington A.C.
29	A. SMITH	" "
30	D. ALEXANDER	Leicester Coritanians
31	P. SIMPSON	Liverpool H.
32	S. JORDAN	Liverpool Pembroke A.C.
33	D. MYTTON	Norwich
34	M. CAMPBELL	Nottingham A.C. (Vet.)
35	G. RICHARDSON	" "
36	B. MIST	Salford University
37	R. THORNTON	Salisbury District A.C.
38	M. GIDDEY	South London H.
39	M. NEWTON	" " "
40	A. RANDALL	" " "
41	D. GOODWIN	Thetford A.C.
42	B. OWEN-JONES	Tipton H.
43	D. GENT (Miss)	Trent Polytechnic
44	T. BURBIDGE	Verlea A.C.
45	J. ATHERTON	Walsall
46	G. HOGGETT	Watford H. (Vet.)
47	M. DAYKIN	Gloucester A.C.
48	D. DOWDLE	" "
49	C. O'CARROLL	" "
50	K. LEYSHON	" "
51	C. DIXON	Unattached (Vet.)
52	D. PERKINS	Kempley A.C.

15

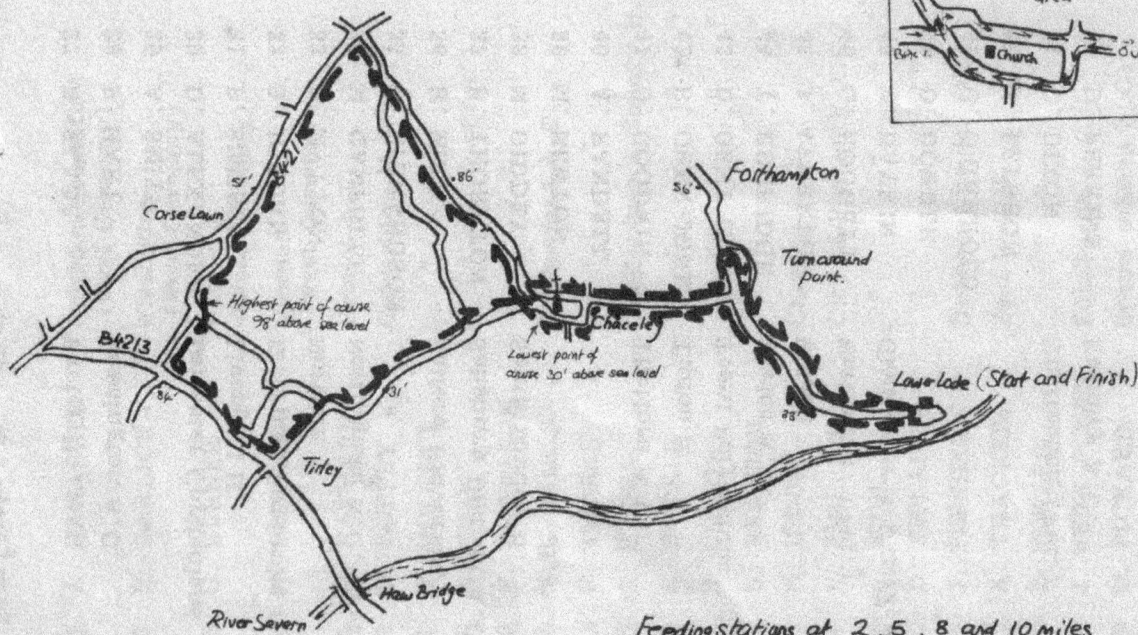

10 X 10MILE LAPS

Enlargement of Chaceley area

ROUTE OF GLOUCESTER 100

The Lower Lode Hotel

FORTHAMPTON, Nr. TEWKESBURY, GLOS.

Telephone : Tewkesbury 293224

SECOND TURNING LEFT OFF THE A438 TEWKESBURY/LEDBURY ROAD
BY RIVER HALF MILE FROM THE BRITISH WATERWAYS UPPER LODE LOCK

All four were regularly running well over four hours every Sunday, Daykin recording 62 miles on one run.

Although all four were the best of friends when not racing, there was no love lost between them when racing, and a lot of local rivalry was building up.

Half of Gloucester were tipping Dowdle to win, while the favourite for the race, Daykin, was hotly tipped to run away with it.

By the end of March, the Gloucester camp knew they were ready for anybody and geared up for a crack at the current world record (held by Don Ritchie of Scotland).

One week to go, everybody was beginning to get keyed up. The week seemed to drag. Then all too soon, Friday night (pre-race night) arrived. The race was due to start at

6 am that Saturday. Friday night turned into food orgy night; anything that had a high carbohydrate content was devoured on sight. The local radio station gave the weather forecast (the one factor which could ruin the race): low cloud, overcast, high temperature, no wind (hooray!). Not perfect weather conditions; there would be a high humidity factor which indicated dehydration problems. The Gloucester squad reckoned on consuming at least four gallons of fluids each for the whole trip.

All drinks were carefully measured, bottled and labelled. Packed away into boxes, ready. Spare shoes, socks, kit, etc., all double-checked and packed. 8 pm, off to bed to grab some sleep. Nobody could sleep, tossing and turning, wondering, finally *dropping off almost, it seemed, just as the alarm goes off at 5 am! No lie-ins today.*

Up, washed, toilet, breakfast, kit quickly checked, packed into the car (enough kit to go on holiday for six months), into the dark unknown. There would be no turning back now.

All are at the start by 5.40 am. "Chris, you there?"

"Yes."

"Martin here?"

"Yes."

"And Ken?"

"Dave?"

"All here okay."

A bit worried about the drinks getting mixed up in the dark. "Don't worry; there is a car to each different feeding station."

Feeding stations every 2 1/2 miles. "Think it's enough?"

"Hope so." Too late now if it isn't.

More and more figures looming out of the dark, constant hubbub of voices, cameras popping, the local TV crew light up the scene as they begin to film. "Five minutes to go," shouts an obscure voice. Give the warm-up a miss! A few easy stretches, back to the toilets again.

"One minute to go, line up please." Timekeepers ready. Watch it now, keep the nerves under control, careful not to end up shooting down the road in a flood of adrenalin, bottle it down, keep calm.

Of the original fifty-one entries, thirty actually lined up for the race. Bang goes the gun. One moment blinded and deafened by the TV lights, cameras, cheers and shouts of the crowd, and the next moment enveloped by the quiet peaceful half-darkness again.

The soft patter of running shoes vanishing into the awakening dawn, the accompaniment of the dawn chorus of birds singing. It didn't remain a peaceful scene for long.

19

THE RACE

⟳ 10 MILES – LAP 1

Straight from the gun, this was a showdown between Daykin and Dowdle of Gloucester. A bunch of four runners, with both Daykin and Dowdle, quickly broke away from the main pack, opening up a gap of half a minute. First 10 miles covered in 67mins 19secs by Daykin, with Dowdle going through in 67mins and 26secs.

Four runners all inside world record schedule.

⟳ 20 MILES – LAP 2

The front bunch were still locked together, Dowdle breathing down Daykin's neck. The main pack a further 13 minutes away. At the 20-mile turn, Daykin is through in 2hrs 14mins and 14secs, Dowdle right alongside, both well inside the world record schedule. Two other Gloucester runners, O'Carroll and Leyshon, through with the main pack in 2hrs 48mins and 06secs. Nothing much happening but still a long, long way to go.

⟳ 30 MILES – LAP 3

Four runners up front, including Daykin and Dowdle. Marathon mark reached in 2hrs 56mins 35secs. Both Gloucester runners together, no quarter given, none asked for. Both clocked in at the 30-mile mark in 3.23.20, with Brown of Cheltenham Harriers and Phillips of the Royal Marines still with them. Well inside world record schedule. Back down the field, Mark Pickard of Epsom and Ewell and Alan Smith of Leamington Spa were in 5th and 6th positions, 3.38.47, with the rest of the field through, the last one in at 5.07.12.

10-mile mark –
Martin Daykin 67.19
Dave Dowdle 67.26

10 miles
Early on in the race with Dave &
Martin ahead of
Steve Brown, Cheltenham
& County Harriers;
Vince Phillips, City of Plymouth AC

*20 miles
Lap 2 – Vince Phillips & Martin
ahead of Dave in lead 20 miles –
Martin 2hrs 14mins 14secs
↻ (Dave and Vince same time)*

*20 miles – Lap 2 Early days –
Ken and Chris just behind the
leaders.*

*Ken and Chris both timed at:
2hrs 48mins 06secs ➲*

30 miles – Lap 3
(far left) Steve Brown, Chelt;
Vince Phillips, Plymouth;
Martin Daykin, Glos

↻ Leading runners with Dave,
Glos just behind

Marathon ran in
2hrs 56mins 35secs

30-mile mark 3hrs 23mins 20secs

(all three runners together)

Dave tracking the leaders
past 30-mile mark

Dave chasing Martin up
to 40-mile mark – 2mins
and behind him both his
brothers on motorbikes
following him.

Bruce Slade of Exeter Harriers having a pit stop at our water station! *"Don't forget to put the sponge back, Bruce. We haven't got that many left."*

Martin's wife, Liz, tracking him ☺

⊃ 40 MILES – LAP 4

Daykin at last made his move. With the temperature rising, Dowdle was stopping to take drinks. A gap quickly opened up. Piling on the pace, Daykin had dropped Dowdle by 2 minutes. The race was on. Daykin clocked in at the 40-mile turn at 4.31.15 to Dowdle's 4.33.29. Next guy in 10 minutes behind. What everybody in the know had expected had now happened. Both Gloucester runners were clear of the field several minutes inside world record schedule. With weather conditions deteriorating and still 60 miles to go, the question was could Daykin maintain his world record pace and resist the challenge of Dowdle?

⊃ 50 MILES – LAP 5

By now, big crowds were beginning to gather at the start of every lap at the hotel. Everyone eagerly waiting to see who would appear on the horizon first. Would it be Daykin with his big aggressive stride and head-rolling action or the economical pitter-patter short striding style of little Dowdle 5ft 5", both instantly recognisable a long way off? Suddenly a cry from the crowd: "Still Daykin in front,"

"Dowdle still there," bigger gap, though.

Daykin swept into the turn, quick stop for drinks, out again, time at 50 miles: 5hrs 42mins and 08 secs; still on for the world record. Dowdle hit the the 50-mile mark in 5.45.57. With cries of "Get after him, Dave" and "Don't let him get away" ringing in his ears, he snatches up drinks bottles in both hands and runs away back up the road, frantically trying to close a 3-minute+ gap.

More cheers from the crowd as the third Gloucester runner, O'Carroll, comes in. He had picked his way up to 6th position; several moments later, the 4th Gloucester runner, Leyshon, was in and out again. People really buzzing now. With the field cut down to twenty-four, four Gloucester runners still in there giving the Gloucestershire crowd plenty to shout about at the halfway stage.

40 miles – Martin made his
break on Lap 4
Martin – through 40 miles in
4hrs 31mins 15secs (2mins
14secs lead over Dave)
Dave – through 40 miles in 4hrs
33mins 29secs

50 miles – Lap 5
Ken & Chris coming in 6th & 7th position

At 50 miles, it was no laughing matter
now; temperatures were getting hotter

Chris – 6hrs 43mins 33secs
Ken – 6hrs 57mins 08secs

(Note the sophisticated cooling system –
can't beat a good bucket and sponge)

⟳ 60 MILES — LAP 6

Air temperature was rising; so was the humidity. It was beginning to wreak havoc on the runners battling against dehydration problems. The three short hills on the course seemed to take on enormous dimensions. The faces of the runners contorted into grimmer outlines as they ran on with the knowledge of 50 miles still to go. All the runners now had to dig deep within themselves for qualities other than sheer physical fitness. Call it heroic courage, stubborn refusal to quit, grittiness; call it what you like, these qualities now had to be drawn out and used to the full. The race to survive was on. Daykin was in trouble; he had slowed off the pace, was taking drinks much more frequently, but Dowdle couldn't do much about it, he too was suffering. 60-mile mark reached by Daykin in 6hrs, 56mins and 12secs, Dowdle in 7hrs, 02mins and 28secs, now past midday. In the next few hours, the temperature would rise again. For the first time, both Gloucester runners were slipping away from the world record schedule – not surprising considering the weather conditions. The race was still very much alive, though. The field was down to just twenty runners. All four Gloucester men still in the race!

60 miles – Lap 6
Liz, Martin's wife, pedalling to the drinks station with more refreshments

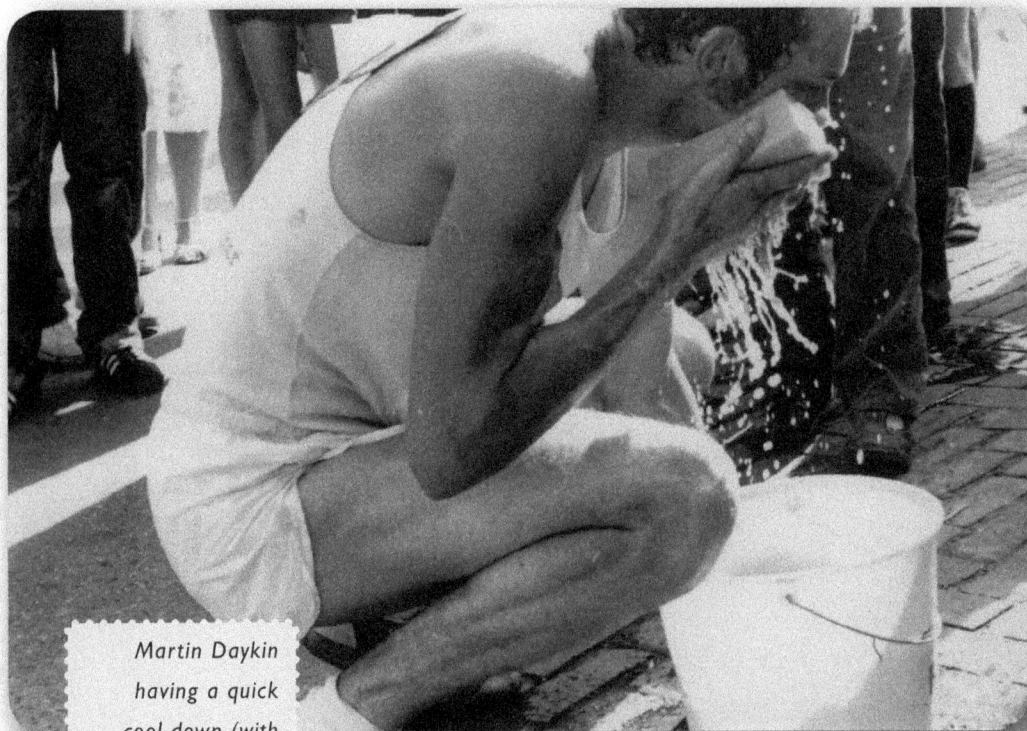

Martin Daykin
having a quick
cool down (with
our state-of-the-
art cooling system
again; lovely)

Johnny Towers of East
Hull Harriors having
a break after going
through 70m mark

⊃ 70 MILES — LAP 7

100km (62 miles), Daykin clocked 7.12.44 with Dowdle past at 7.19.42, 3rd place Pickard of Epsom and Ewell at 8.04.30. Daykin was now going through a really bad patch. His wife, Liz, by now accompanying her husband on her bicycle, realised he was dehydrating rapidly; pedalling furiously to the next feeding station, grabbing all the drinks she could, she pedalled back to her husband to give him the life-saving fluids. People began to worry in the Gloucester camp. Had he gone too fast?

Considering the conditions, nobody could help him. He was on his own. Dowdle began to close. At the turn, the crowd suddenly erupted, Daykin weaving from side to side, staggering in. Almost hidden behind the large frame of Daykin came Dowdle. He had closed up to only 2 1/2 minutes behind. Daykin collapsed into a chair muttering to himself, his head buried into his chest. A towel was quickly draped across his shoulders. He just sat there not moving at all, unable to. The crowd fell deadly silent. Surely Daykin wasn't calling it a day, not one of the most feared ultra-distance runners in Europe (ranked No. 1 at 100km in world rankings in 1981)? Daykin's time at 70 miles, 8.19.39. Dowdle's time, 8.22.18.

With Daykin stopped dead, Dowdle now seized his chance; another quick pit stop for drinks and away to the cheers of the crowd into the lead for the first time, running for all he was worth, trying to open up as big a gap as possible. Both Daykin's parents and his wife frantically tried to get him back on his feet again, cajoled him, shouted at him, and all manner of drinks were given to him – even a couple of beers! After what seemed an eternity (but only about 10 minutes), he got to his feet. With the crowd and his wife, Liz, yelling encouragement to him, he started running again. Big sighs of relief from the crowd. The crowd was soon to be on its feet again as Gloucester's 3rd and 4th runners, O'Carroll and Leyshon, both went through. So at the 70-mile mark, incredibly, there were still four Gloucester runners in the race out of only seventeen left standing.

⊃ 80 MILES — LAP 8

With all the drama of the last lap, people were really breathless. Dowdle was now in the lead, trying all he knew to increase it. The temperature, thank God, was now beginning to drop, but Daykin wasn't going to drop! He began to work on the gap between himself and Dowdle, looking a lot fresher than he did on the last lap.

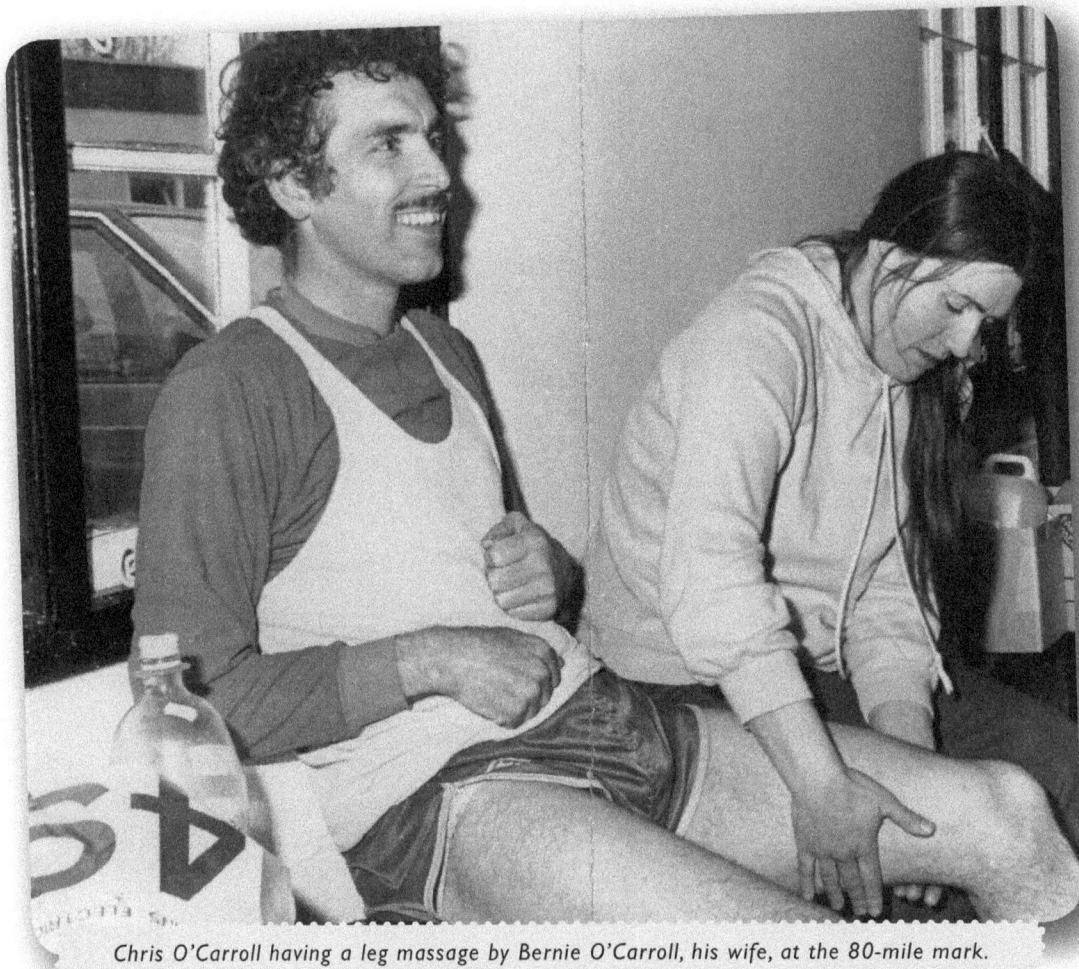

Chris O'Carroll having a leg massage by Bernie O'Carroll, his wife, at the 80-mile mark. "Hurry up, Bernie! I need a miracle here!" I did! Ended up in a nearby hospital with dehydration and hypothermia after completing the 100-mile race

At the 90-mile mark, I ran the last 10 miles surprisingly fast! With the weather going from red hot all day, to very cold at night-time, I should have in hindsight stopped, put on a warm change of clothes and had a lot of warm drinks; probably wouldn't have got into the situation above had I done this. I sprinted into the finish and then fell down... there's a lesson learned!

Dowdle was still holding on to his lead as he came into the turn at the 80-mile mark, 09hrs, 37mins and 07secs. No sooner was the time announced than all eyes swept up the road again as Daykin came thundering in. "He's closed the gap," gasped the crowd. Dowdle couldn't believe it. Ten miles earlier, he had left a lifeless Daykin limp on a chair. He had run himself into the deck to get away and here was Daykin back again, clocking in at 09hrs 39mins and 10secs. Only 2 minutes 3 seconds behind him! No time to waste, Dowdle was up and off, face grimacing with the sustained effort of trying all he knew to keep his hard-earned lead. Looking anxiously over his shoulder, his heart nearly stopped; Daykin was after him, no long rest this time. He was doing a Dowdle, a drinks bottle in each hand and off up the road. What a race! 80 miles covered and both Gloucester runners in a neck-and-neck struggle; world-class times were on too. With only 20 miles still to go, would one or the other blow up? Would they run each other into the deck? The crowd could hardly contain its excitement. Some of the local inhabitants who had never seen a road race or such scenes before just couldn't believe what was happening. One local, when informed about the 100- mile road race, had asked what kind of cars they were using!

With constant press and radio coverage, people were beginning to gather at every vantage point, roar after roar of encouragement going up as runner after runner struggled on. Incredibly, four Gloucester runners were still in there trading punches. Sixteen runners only now remained.

Coming up to Lap 8 — 80-mile mark Martin is in trouble!
Martin's wife, Liz, rushing to get more fluids for him!

Martin, assisted by his mum to get to a chair and get some fluids into him, to rehydrate! Worried brother and his dad looking on! Up to 10-minute pit stop!

➲ 90 MILES — LAP 9

Could such drama and scenes go on? Several runners were running themselves into road-running history. Another chapter to add to road-running folklore. Word came back by radio that Daykin was ahead again. At the drinks stop at 87 1/2 miles, Dowdle had again passed Daykin – ahead for the second time and so it was at the turn. Dowdle was still there, sweat-stricken face glancing over his shoulder. Daykin loomed larger than life, it seemed, behind him. Dowdle hit the 90-mile marker, a deafening reception, in 10 hours, 56 minutes and 08 seconds. Daykin was in at 10 hours, 58 minutes and 10 seconds. Dowdle had held him at bay and only lost a second on the last lap. Like two boxers coming out for the last round, thundering body blows into each other, they set off on their last lap. The strain on both crowd and runners was immense!

➲ 100 MILES — LAP 10

Yet again the crowds were erupting into great roars of encouragement; Daykin was slowly pulling Dowdle back before their very eyes, yard after agonising yard.

Dowdle, his head up, gasping for air, refusing to give up either to himself or anybody. Daykin, teeth clenched, body rolling, saying to himself over and over again, got to keep the stride pattern, keep the length, trying to ignore the agonising ache in his thighs and calves. Both runners by now accompanied by cars with headlights blazing, horns blowing, with cavalcades of cars, bikes and runners behind and in front. Dowdle's lead was being cut still shorter: 300, 200, 150, 50 yards, level. Neck and neck again. Dowdle responds, but Daykin refuses to let go. Four incredible miles to go. A supreme battle of wills was now going on out there. Who dares wins! Two miles to go, Daykin in front... just!

With one mile to go, Daykin makes a supreme effort. Dowdle couldn't respond to it; 25-, 39-, 50-, 75-yard gap. Daykin swaying and rolling turns for home, not daring to look back. The noise is enough to tell him. The noise gets louder, Dowdle coming back at him. Daykin responds to hold the gap. 300 yards to go; Daykin spots the finish first and pounds down to it.

Dowdle turns for home and starts sprinting, to everyone's amazement. Just cannot believe it. Daykin, with only 200 yards to go, has got to fight for his life. After 99 miles 1,565 yards, he has still got to try to fight off this 26-year-old terrier Dowdle, who just won't quit. Throwing his head back, arms and legs pumping with one last-ditch effort, Daykin maintains the gap, crashes over the line and collapses in a heap.

Dowdle crosses the line into a tearful mother overcome by the whole affair. Daykin's time: an incredible 12 hours, 16 minutes and 46 seconds. Dowdle: 12 hours, 17 minutes and 09 seconds. A mere 23-seconds difference bore witness to one of the most enthralling ultra-distance road races ever.

Nearly two hours later, the 3rd place runner finishes: Dave Goodwin of Thetford Harriers, in a world-class time of 14 hours, 07 minutes and 42 seconds; 4th was Mark Pickford of Epsom and Ewell in a time of 14 hours, 13 minutes and 50 seconds; 5th to finish was John Towers of East Hull Harriers, 14 hours, 21 minutes and 01 second; 6th, Chris O'Carroll, 3rd Gloucester runner, 15 hours, 21 minutes and 07 seconds. To complete Gloucester's day, their 4th runner, Ken Leyshon, completed the course in 16 hours, 25 minutes and 08 seconds. Only thirteen runners finished.

Amid all the noise and confusion, the timekeepers were still going about their expert business and came up with the following results.

1st	Martin Daykin	Gloucester A.C.	12hrs 16mins 46secs (English Record) 2nd all time world best
2nd	Dave Dowdle	Gloucester A.C.	12hrs 17mins 09secs (3rd all time world best)
3rd	Dave Goodwin	Thetford AC	14hrs 07mins 42secs (20th all time world best)
4th	Mark Pickard	Epsom and Ewell	14hrs 13mins 50secs (21st all time world best)
5th	John Towers	East Hull Terriers	14hrs 21mins 01secs (23rd all time world best)
6th	Chris O'Carroll	Gloucester A.C.	15hrs 21mins 07secs (33rd all time world best)
7th	Bruce Slade	Exeter Harriers	15hrs 38mins 34secs (39th all time world best)
8th	Steve Jordan	Liverpool	15hrs 43mins 41secs (15th all time British best)
9th	Colin Dixon	Unatached	16hrs 19mins 42secs (16th all time British best)
10th	Ken Leyshon	Gloucester A.C.	16hrs 25mins 08secs (17th all time British best)
11th	Alan Smith	Leamington AC	17hrs 16mins 11secs (20th all time British best)
12th	Malcolm Campbell	Notts AC	17hrs 18mins 28secs (21st all time British best)
13th	Ken Shaw	Cambridge Harriers	17hrs 48mins 37secs

Martin finishing 100-mile race in 1st position (second fastest time in the world on road 100 miles, fastest Englander ever)

Dave finishing 100-mile race in 2nd position (third fastest 100-mile runner in the world on the road, second fastest Englander)

Quietly reflecting on the race later, the four Gloucester runners admitted that mistakes were made and valuable lessons learned by all.

But who would have guessed that that informal meeting back in December 1980 would result in Gloucester Athletic club proudly boasting on 12 April 1981 one of the most powerful ultra-distance running squads in Europe? The Gloucester squad hope to be going over to the States sometime in the future and will be seen in action in Europe later this year. They now have a proud reputation to keep up. No doubt we shall be hearing a lot more from them in the future.

➲ AFTER-RACE COMMENTS

Martin Daykin: Ready to quit at 70 miles, knew world record wasn't on, but how could I pack in with three Gloucester club mates still running? I would have had to emigrate if I had quit.

Dave Dowdle: Thought I had the race sewn up 20 out. Still, first attempt. Can't believe I'm suddenly 3rd fastest ever in the world! With better weather conditions and a flatter course next time out, sub-12 is on, even the record!

1st by 23 seconds –
Martin Daykin

2nd, Dave Dowdle – "Perhaps I should have skipped the tea and had a beer like Martin."

Chris O'Carroll: I ran and watched a great race by my two club mates in front. It was only when they had finished, I realised I had to do a bit myself to finish. Pleased with finishing 6th, time a bit slow, though… Have to knock an hour or two off it next time out.

Ken Leyshon: First half, okay; second half, suffering with badly swollen and blistered feet. No way was I quitting, not with three of my club mates all finishing. Have to be better equipped and prepared next time. Proud we all finished in one piece.

Liz & Martin after the race finished

Dave with his mum after the race was over!

Martin congratulating
Dave on his run

Martin and Dave having a chat with a young Pat Overthrow of Gloucester AC. Pat was part of a whole raft of helpers from Glos AC, who all helped us!

Host of the Lower Lode Hotel, Forthampton, Glos – Martin and Dave having a
well-earned pint or two, or three, or four… I don't remember

Martin and Liz reminiscing
after the race

Martin receiving his winner's trophy for 100-mile road race
with a young Mark Pickard looking on

Dave collecting his runner-up's prize for 100-mile road race,
with Alan Smith from Leamington AC looking on

Mark Pickard receiving his own award in 4th position in 14hrs 13mins 50secs

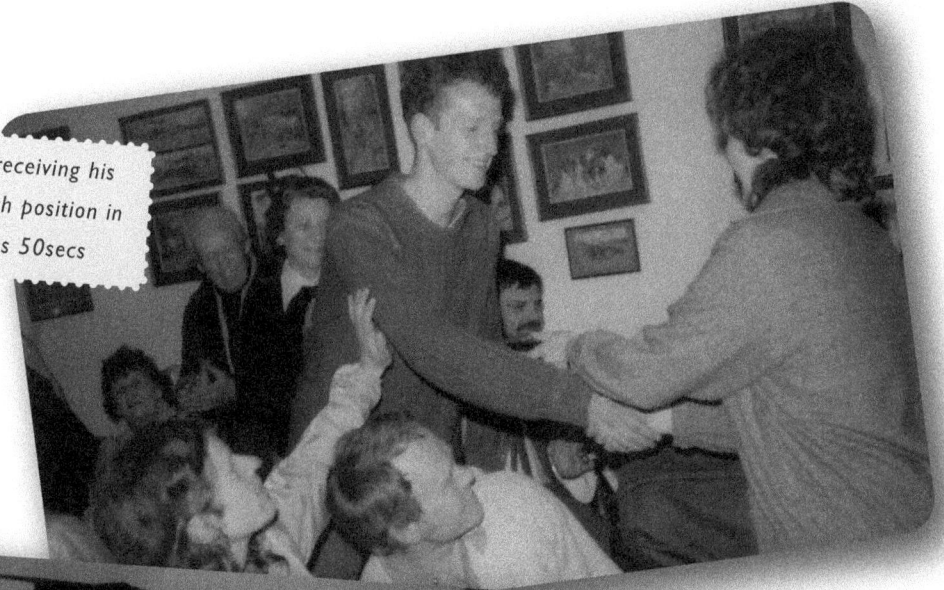

Bruce Slade, Exeter AC; Steve McHale, Glos AC & Ken Leyshon, Glos AC at the 100-mile Awards

Malcolm Cambell, Notts AC finishing in 12th position - 17hrs 18mins 28secs Receiving his trophy.

INTERMEDIATE TIMES

	10 Miles			20 Miles			Marathon	
1	Daykin	1.07.19	1	Daykin	2.14.14	1	Daykin	2.56.35
2	Brown	1.07.19	2	Brown	2.14.14	2	Brown	2.56.35
3	Phillips	1.07.19	3	Phillips	2.14.14	3	Phillips	2.56.35
4	Dowdle	1.07.28	4	Dowdle	2.14.14	4	Dowdle	2.56.35
5	Slade	1.15.02	5	Smith	2.27.51	5	Smith	3.12.00
6	Pickard	1.16.23	6	Pickard	2.27.51	6	Pickard	3.12.00
7	Smith	1.16.23	7	Slade	2.30.22	7	Slade	3.23.00
8	Burbidge	1.17.16	8	Burbidge	2.35.02	8	Goodwin	3.24.00
9	Goodwin	1.18.44	9	Goodwin	2.36.45	9	Towers	3.24.00
10	Towers	1.18.44	10	Towers	2.36.46	10	Burbidge	3.25.00
11	Mytton	1.21.45	11	Simpson	2.40.20	11	Simpson	3.30.00
12	Simpson	1.21.48	12	Mytton	2.41.26	12	Mytton	3.31.00
13	Dixon	1.21.52	13	Hoggett	2.43.14	13	Dixon	3.33.00
14	Hoggett	1.22.06	14	Dixon	2.44.00	14	Buckle	3.35.00
15	Buckle	1.24.14	15	Randall	2.46.47	15	Heaford	3.35.00
16	Heaford	1.24.14	16	Turner	2.46.47	16	Randall	3.36.00
17	Leyshon	1.24.47	17	Buckle	2.47.08	17	Turner	3.36.00
18	O'Carroll	1.24.47	18	Campbell	2.47.14	18	Leyshon	3.37.00
19	Turner	1.25.00	19	Heaford	2.47.22	19	O'Carroll	3.37.00
20	Randall	1.25.00	20	Leyshon	2.48.05	20	Campbell	3.37.00
21	Hayward	1.25.00	21	O'Carroll	2.48.06	21	Hoggett	3.40.00
22	Thornton	1.25.36	22	Hayward	2.51.43	22	Hayward	3.45.00
23	Soul	1.26.30	23	Tiplady	2.52.38	23	Soul	3.47.00
24	Campbell	1.26.48	24	Soul	2.52.40	24	Tiplady	3.52.00
25	Shaw	1.26.51	25	Werner	2.55.36	25	Werner	3.52.00
26	Tiplady	1.28.06	26	Jordan	2.58.30	26	Jordan	3.54.00
27	Werner	1.28.06	27	Thornton	2.58.30	27	Thornton	3.56.00
28	Alexander	1.28.07	28	Alexander	2.59.00	28	Shaw	3.56.00
29	Jordan	1.28.07	29	Shaw	2.59.25	29	Alexander	4.05.00
30	Richardson	1.36.53	30	Richardson	3.21.40	30	Richardson	4.30.00

	30 Miles			40 Miles			50 Miles	
1	Daykin	3.23.20	1	Daykin	4.31.15	1	Daykin	5.42.08
2	Brown	3.23.20	2	Dowdle	4.33.29	2	Dowdle	5.45.57
3	Dowdle	3.23.21	3	Phillips	4.43.53	3	Pickard	6.11.00
4	Phillips	3.23.24	4	Pickard	4.54.08	4	Goodwin	6.30.35
5	Pickard	3.38.47	5	Smith	4.59.00	5	Towers	6.34.08
6	Smith	3.38.47	6	Goodwin	5.13.48	6	O'Carroll	6.43.33
7	Towers	3.54.40	7	Towers	5.14.24	7	Smith	6.46.14
8	Slade	3.54.48	8	Slade	5.21.24	8	Slade	6.51.47
9	Goodwin	3.54.48	9	Buckle	5.22.14	9	Leyshon	6.57.08
10	Burbidge	3.59.10	10	Mytton	5.24.15	10	Dixon	6.59.12
11	Simpson	4.01.10	11	O'Carroll	5.24.04	11	Mytton	7.10.52
12	Mytton	4.02.24	12	Leyshon	5.25.04	12	Randall	7.11.52
13	Dixon	4.02.34	13	Dixon	5.25.59	13	Campbell	7.22.43
14	Buckle	4.05.28	14	Randall	5.35.58	14	Hayward	7.30.30
15	Heaford	4.05.28	15	Burbidge	5.39.25	15	Jordan	7.30.30
16	Leyshon	4.05.40	16	Campbell	5.41.15	16	Werner	7.42.24
17	O'Carroll	4.05.40	17	Heaford	5.45.00	17	Burbidge	7.48.30
18	Turner	4.06.58	18	Hayward	5.49.18	18	Shaw	7.54.47
19	Randall	4.07.00	19	Simpson	5.58.07	19	Hoggett	8.03.40
20	Campbell	4.09.20	20	Tiplady	5.58.52	20	Tiplady	8.04.20
21	Hoggett	4.17.54	21	Jordan	5.59.02	21	Soul	8.06.24
22	Hayward	4.18.52	22	Soul	5.59.24	22	Heaford	8.53.20
23	Soul	4.21.00	23	Werner	5.59.55	23	Richardson	9.35.27
24	Tiplady	4.21.25	24	Hoggett	6.01.31			
25	Werner	4.26.25	25	Shaw	6.11.33			
26	Jordan	4.28.06	26	Richardson	7.04.40			
27	Shaw	4.32.06						
28	Thornton	4.32.06						
29	Alexander	5.04.58						
30	Richardson	5.07.12						

60 Miles			100 kms.			70 Miles	
1	Daykin	6.56.12	1	Daykin	7.12.44	1	Daykin	8.19.39
2	Dowdle	7.02.28	2	Dowdle	7.19.42	2	Dowdle	8.21.18
3	Pickard	7.41.54	3	Pickard	8.04.30	3	Pickard	9.26.10
4	Towers	8.01.10	4	Towers	8.21.00	4	Goodwin	9.32.00
5	Goodwin	8.04.08	5	Goodwin	8.26.43	5	Towers	9.32.15
6	O'Carroll	8.14.16	6	O'Carroll	8.43.12	6	O'Carroll	9.56.20
7	Slade	8.21.12	7	Slade	8.54.48	7	Slade	10.15.58
8	Dixon	8.33.32	8	Dixon	8.55.55	8	Dixon	10.20.18
9	Smith	8.40.55	9	Smith	9.03.30	9	Smith	10.20.22
10	Campbell	8.55.00	10	Campbell	9.17.16	10	Leyshon	10.38.40
11	Leyshon	9.00.22	11	Leyshon	9.21.30	11	Jordan	10.48.04
12	Jordan	9.14.21	12	Jordan	9.35.23	12	Campbell	10.57.31
13	Randall	9.20.54	13	Shaw	10.09.52	13	Shaw	11.34.03
14	Werner	9.36.14	14	Werner	10.10.24	14	Werner	11.44.00
15	Hayward	9.40.18	15	Hayward	10.06.22	15	Hayward	11.45.54
16	Shaw	9.43.08	16	Mytton	10.14.04	16	Hoggett	12.18.05
17	Mytton	9.43.38	17	Burbidge	10.28.56	17	Tiplady	12.45.25
18	Burbidge	9.57.43	18	Hoggett	10.46.05			
19	Hoggett	10.13.30						
20	Tiplady	10.19.23						

80 Miles			90 Miles			100 Miles		
1	Dowdle	9.37.07	1	Dowdle	10.56.08	1	Daykin	12.16.46
2	Daykin	9.39.10	2	Daykin	10.58.10	2	Dowdle	12.17.09
3	Goodwin	10.58.48	3	Goodwin	12.38.00	3	Goodwin	14.07.42
4	Pickard	11.06.06	4	Pickard	12.45.56	4	Pickard	14.13.50
5	Towers	11.11.35	5	Towers	12.50.09	5	Towers	14.21.01
6	O'Carroll	11.50.05	6	O'Carroll	13.33.39	6	O'Carroll	15.21.07
7	Slade	12.10.06	7	Slade	13.54.45	7	Slade	15.38.34
8	Dixon	12.13.22	8	Jordan	14.02.00	8	Jordan	15.43.41
9	Leyshon	12.17.00	9	Leyshon	14.05.11	9	Dixon	16.19.42
10	Jordan	12.26.20	10	Dixon	14.07.22	10	Leyshon	16.25.08
11	Campbell	12.49.10	11	Smith	14.37.15	11	Smith	17.16.11
12	Smith	12.55.19	12	Campbell	14.52.16	12	Campbell	17.18.28
13	Shaw	13.26.32	13	Shaw	15.32.41	13	Shaw	17.48.37
14	Hayward	14.04.34	14	Hayward	16.23.46			
15	Werner	14.21.32	15	Tiplady	17.35.10			
16	Tiplady	15.07.55						

11th April, 1981.

GLOUCESTER 100
100 MILE ROAD RACE

RESULTS

1	M.DAYKIN	(GLOUCESTER A.C.)	12:16:46
2	D.DOWDLE	(GLOUCESTER A.C.)	12:17:09
3	D.GOODWIN	(THETFORD A.C.)	14:07:42
4	M.PICKARD	(EPSOM & EWELL A.C.)	14:13:50
5	J.TOWERS	(EAST HULL HARRIERS)	14:21:01
6	C.O'CARROLL	(GLOUCESTER A.C.)	15:21:07
7	B.SLADE	(EXETER HARRIERS)	15:38:34
8	S.JORDAN	(LIVERPOOL PEMBROKE)	15:43:41
9	C.DIXON	(UNATTACHED)	16:19:42
10	K.LEYSHON	(GLOUCESTER A.C.)	16:25:08
11	A.SMITH	(LEAMINGTON A.C.)	17:16:11
12	M.CAMPBELL	(NOTTINGHAM A.C.)	17:18:28
13	K.SHAW	(CAMBRIDGE HARRIERS)	17:48:37
14	D.HAYWARD	(BRISTOL A.C.)	90 MILES
15	D.TIPLADY	(CITY OF PLYMOUTH)	90 MILES
16	G.WERNER	(BANBERG, W.GERMANY)	80 MILES
17	G.HOGGETT	(WATFORD HARRIERS)	70 MILES
18	D.MYTTON	(NORWICH)	100 KMS.
19	T.BURBIDGE	(VERLEA A.C.)	100 KMS.
20	A.RANDALL	(SOUTH LONDON H.)	60 MILES
21	R.SOUL	(CITY OF PLYMOUTH)	50 MILES
22	B.HEAFORD	(CHELTENHAM & CTY. H.)	50 MILES
23	G.RICHARDSON	(NOTTINGHAM A.C.)	50 MILES
24	V.PHILLIPS	(CITY OF PLYMOUTH)	40 MILES
25	K.BUCKLE	(CHELTENHAM & CTY. H)	40 MILES
26	P.SIMPSON	(LIVERPOOL HARRIERS)	40 MILES
27	S.BROWN	(CHELTENHAM & CTY. H)	30 MILES
28	D.TURNER	(EPSOM & EWELL A.C.)	30 MILES
29	R.THORNTON	(SALISBURY DISTRICT)	30 MILES
30	D.ALEXANDER	(LEICESTER CORITANIANS)	30 MILES

FOR ALL YOU FEENTS, THE STATISTICS FREAKS *(handwritten)*

****

RACE LEADERS

START TO 30 MILES	:	DAYKIN, DOWDLE, PHILLIPS, AND BROWN
30 TO 70 MILES	:	DAYKIN
70 TO 83 MILES	:	DOWDLE
83 TO 88 MILES	:	DAYKIN
88 TO 93 MILES	:	DOWDLE
93 TO 100MILES	:	DAYKIN

TEN X 10 MILE CIRCUITS.

LOWEST POINT OF COURSE - 30 FEET ABOVE SEA LEVEL.
HIGHEST POINT   - 98 "   "   "   "

REVISED   100 Miles Road All-time List   *AFTER THE RACE*

1.	11:51:12	Don Ritchie (Forres)	15.6.79	Flushing Meadow N.J.
2.	12:16:46	Martin Daykin (Gloucester A.C)	11.4.81	Forthampton Glos.
3.	12:17:09	Dave Dowdle (Gloucester A.C.)	11.4.81	Forthampton Glos.
4.	12:18:16	Ron Hopcroft (Thames Valley)	25.10.58	Hyde Pk. Corner-Box.
5.	12:20:28	Wally Hayward (South Africa)	24.10.53	Box-Hyde Pk. Corner.
6.	12:54:31	Jose Cortez (United States)	13.3.71	Rocklin California.
7.	12:55:12	Mike Newton (Sth. London H.)	26.7.80	Forest Green.
8.	13:04:09	Stu Mittleman (United States)	13.6.80	Flushing Meadow N.J.
9.	13:08:36	Jackie Mekler (South Africa)	24.10.53	Box-Hyde Pk. Corner.
10.	13:13:46	Len Keating (Rhodesia)	7.78	E.London-Port Alfred.
11.	13:17:38	Arthur Mail (Derby C.A.C.)	24.10.59	Walton.
12.	13:21:00	Max Telford (New Zealand)	76	Hawaii.
13.	13:21:19	Hardy Ballington (Sth. Africa)	2.7.37	Box-Hyde Pk. Corner.
14.	13:33:46	Lion Caldwell (United States)	15.6.79	New Jersey.
15.	13:36:35	Don Marvel (United States)	13.6.80	New Jersey.
16.	13:40:50	Fred Squitz (United States)	13.6.80	New Jersey.
17.	13:43:54	Don Turner (Epsom & Ewell)	24.10.59	Walton.
18.	13:47:18	Derek Reynolds (Blackheath)	24.10.53	Box-Hyde Pk. Corner
19.	13:57:35	Park Barner (United States)	24.6.78	New Jersey.
20.	14:07:42	Dave Goodwin (Thetford A.C.)	11.4.81	Forthampton.
21.	14:13:50	Mark Pickard (Epsom & Ewell)	11.4.81	Forthampton.
22.	14:14:39	Ken Young (United States)	11.3.72	Sacramento.
23.	14:21:01	John Towers (East Hull H.)	11.4.81	Forthampton.
24.	14:22:10	Arthur Newton (Rhodesia)	7.1.28	Box-Hyde Pk. Corner.
25.	14:30:05	Cahiti Yetre (Turkey)	24.6.78	New Jersey.
26.	14:32:59	Steve Jordan (Liverpool Pem.)	27.7.80	Forest Green.
27.	14:37:04	Nick Marshall (United States)	24.6.78	New Jersey.
28.	14:42:59	Paul Ryan (United States)	26.5.79	Hawaii.
29.	14:51:12	Dave Obelkevitch (U.S.A.)	13.6.70	New Jersey.
30.	14:53:45	Denis Stephenson (New Z.)	64	Auckland.
31.	15:08:02	Brian Jones (United States)	24.6.78	New Jersey.
32.	15:13:43	Bill McCray (United States)	8.3.75	Sacramento.
33.	15:21:07	Chris O'Carroll (Gloucester)	11.4.81	Forthampton.
34.	15:22:26*	Leslie Pocock (Reading A.C.)	16.7.54	Brighton-London & back.
35.	15:23:47	Tammie Bilibana (Sth. Africa)	27.6.80	E.London-Port Alfred.
36.	15:23:51	Don Underwood (South Africa)	6/7.7.79	E.London-Port Alfred.
37.	15:25:30	George Gardiner (U.S.A.)	13.6.80	New Jersey.
38.	15:37:22	Bill Lawder (United States)	24.6.78	New Jersey.
39.	15:38:34	Bruce Slade (Exeter Harriers)	11.4.81	Forthampton.
40.	15:38:38	Darryl Beardall (U.S.A.)	11.3.72	Sacramento.
41.	15:40:02	D. Parks (South Africa)	6/7.7.79	E.London-Port Alfred.

*Time at 104m. 1130yds.

Uncertain as to road or track:

15:17:22	Frank Bozanich (U.S.A.)	14.6.80	Virginia.
15:23:37	Doug Wood (New Zealand)	68	Dunedin.

British Road 100 Mile Marks Outside 16 Hours

16.	16:19:42	Colin Dixon (Hull-unattached)	11.4.81	Forthampton.
17.	16:25:08	Ken Leyshon (Gloucester A.C.)	11.4.81	Forthampton.
18.	16:44:51	Ken Jordan (Holmfirth H.)	26.7.80	Forest Green.
19.	16:49:58	Ken Shaw (Cambridge Harriers)	26.7.80	Forest Green.
20.	17:16:11	Alan Smith (Leamington A.C.)	11.4.81	Forthampton.
21.	17:18:28	Malcolm Campbell (Notts. A.C.)	11.4.81	Forthampton
22.	17:22:40	Aubrey Parsons	24.10.59	Walton.

* * * * * * * * * *

The above statistics kindly supplied by Andy Milroy

4 GLOS AC LADS IN TOP TWENTY

STAGE TIMES

	10M.	20M.	30M.	40M.	50M.	60M.	70M.	80M.	90M.	100M.
1. Daykin	1.07.19	1.06.55	1.09.06	1.07.55	1.10.53	1.14.04	1.23.27	1.19.31	1.19.00	1.18.36
2. Brown	1.07.19	1.06.55	1.09.06	-	-	-	-	-	-	-
3. Phillips	1.07.19	1.06.55	1.09.10	1.20.29	-	-	-	-	-	-
4. Dowdle	1.07.28	1.06.46	1.09.47	1.10.08	1.12.28	1.16.31	1.18.50	1.16.49	1.19.01	1.21.01
5. Slade	1.15.02	1.15.20	1.24.26	1.26.36	1.30.23	1.33.25	1.50.46	1.54.08	1.44.39	1.43.49
6. Pickard	1.16.23	1.11.28	1.18.56	1.15.21	1.16.52	1.30.54	1.46.16	1.39.54	1.39.50	1.27.54
7. Smith	1.16.23	1.11.26	1.18.56	1.20.13	1.47.14	1.54.41	1.39.27	2.34.57	1.41.56	2.38.56
8. Burbidge	1.17.16	1.17.46	1.24.08	1.40.15	2.09.05	2.09.13	-	-	-	-
9. Goodwin	1.18.44	1.18.01	1.18.03	1.19.00	1.16.47	1.33.33	1.27.52	1.26.48	1.39.12	1.29.42
10. Towers	1.18.44	1.18.02	1.18.02	1.19.36	1.19.44	1.27.02	1.31.05	1.39.20	1.38.34	1.30.52
11. Mytton	1.21.45	1.19.41	1.20.58	1.21.51	1.46.37	2.32.46	-	-	-	-
12. Simpson	1.21.48	1.18.32	1.20.50	1.56.57	-	-	-	-	-	-
13. Dixon	1.21.52	1.22.08	1.18.34	1.23.25	1.33.13	1.34.20	1.46.46	1.53.04	1.54.00	2.12.20
14. Hoggett	1.22.06	1.21.08	1.34.40	1.43.37	2.02.09	2.09.50	2.04.35	-	-	-
15. Buckle	1.24.14	1.22.54	1.18.20	1.16.46	-	-	-	-	-	-
16. Heaford	1.24.14	1.23.08	1.18.06	1.39.32	3.08.20	-	-	-	-	-
17. Leyshon	1.24.47	1.23.18	1.17.35	1.19.24	1.32.04	2.03.14	1.38.18	1.38.20	1.48.11	2.19.57
18. O'Carroll	1.24.47	1.23.19	1.17.34	1.19.24	1.18.29	1.31.43	1.42.04	1.53.45	1.43.34	1.47.28
19. Turner	1.25.00	1.21.47	1.20.11	-	-	-	-	-	-	-
20. Randall	1.25.00	1.21.47	1.20.13	1.28.58	1.35.54	2.09.02	-	-	-	-
21. Hayward	1.25.00	1.26.43	1.27.09	1.30.26	1.41.12	2.09.48	2.05.36	2.18.40	2.19.12	-
22. Thornton	1.25.36	1.32.54	1.33.56	-	-	-	-	-	-	-
23. Soul	1.26.30	1.26.10	1.28.20	1.38.24	2.07.00	-	-	-	-	-
24. Campbell	1.26.48	1.20.26	1.21.06	1.21.55	1.41.28	1.32.17	2.02.31	1.51.39	2.03.06	2.26.12
25. Shaw	1.26.51	1.32.34	1.32.41	1.39.27	1.43.14	1.48.21	1.50.57	1.52.27	2.06.09	2.15.56
26. Tiplady	1.28.06	1.24.32	1.28.47	1.37.27	2.05.28	2.15.03	2.26.02	2.22.30	2.27.15	-
27. Werner	1.28.06	1.27.30	1.30.49	1.33.30	1.42.29	1.53.80	2.07.46	2.37.32	-	-
28. Alexander	1.28.07	1.30.53	2.05.58	-	-	-	-	-	-	-
29. Jordan	1.28.07	1.30.23	1.29.36	1.30.56	1.31.28	1.43.51	1.33.43	1.38.16	1.35.40	1.41.41
30. Richardson	1.36.53	1.44.47	1.45.32	1.56.28	2.30.47	-	-	-	-	-

Must mention Christine Barrett, a housewife from Gloucester. While we were competing in our ultra-distance races in the 1980s, Christine was into triathlons, including the Ironman Triathlon in Hawaii and other places around the world.

Christine competed in the Gloucester AC second 100-mile 1984 road race and set a world record time! Beating the old record by 22 minutes. Recording a time of 15 hours 7 minutes. A great result!

My only regret was that she didn't compete with the Gloucester AC squad earlier. What a team we would have had!

Christine on top of the world

By Peter Savidge

BROCKWORTH'S Christine Barrett collapsed in a heap at the end of Saturday's 100-mile road race near Tewkesbury and well she might . . . she had just run that distance faster than any other woman.

She chopped 22 minutes off the previous world record, held by American Donna Hudson, to finish the race in 15 hours, seven minutes.

Christine said: "I picked up a couple of injuries before the race, the first after competing in a triathlon in October. I had to take two months off to recover.

"Then three weeks ago pulled a hamstring. Fortunately, the healed quickly."

Those disruptions meant she had been able to put in only two long runs before Saturday, one of 39 miles the other 34.

Compared with Saturday those two must have seemed like a sprint to the corner shop.

"The longest distance I have ever run before, was 53 miles.

That was in last year's London to Brighton race, so I really did not know what to expect on Saturday," she said.

Things went well for the Brockworth housewife. She made a fast start and at one point was on schedule to better the record by a huge three hours.

With the sun brilliant at midday, there was a fear she might have started too quickly.

Christine later explained the heat was only a minor problem. Her triathlon experience, including trips to the world championships in Hawaii, have helped her acclimatise to strong sunlight.

"Toughest part was the last five miles. It took me 56 minutes to reach the finish."

Dave Dowdle of Longlevens failed in his record attempt. He had been on schedule after the first 35 miles, but then tired as the temperature rose.

But he still managed first place overall. His finishing time of 13 hours, 10 minutes, 10 seconds was the eighth fastest.

Cheltenham's Bob Hamilton was third in 16 hours, two minutes, 26 seconds . . . Christine Barrett taking second.

Of Gloucester's three other runners, Bill Weller dropped out after 55 miles, Ken Layshon after 50 and John Howe, 50.

CITIZEN 16th APRIL 1984

Christine Barrett . . . record run

Our thanks again to all who helped and supported us, to produce a great 100-mile race! Thanks to the race officials, timekeepers, special mention to Don Turner (Grade 1 timekeeper) from RRC Great Britain, along with our Gloucester timekeepers, who did a fantastic job!

Thanks to Gloucester Athletics Club, who were behind us all the way!

Back down to earth, with a couple of weeks' easy jogging to recover both physically and mentally, Martin was slowly building up to a marathon + a day. Running to work and back from his home in the Kemply area, over trail and road around May Hill, near Huntly, on into Gloucester and back home most days over hilly terrain.

Dave, Ken and myself, who lived in Gloucester, were also building up the mileage, mostly 10 miles in the morning and 16 miles in the evening (marathon + a day) over hilly terrain. Running from Gloucester, through Upton St Leonards, up to the Portway (1mile uphill), over to Sheepscombe (second steep hill), left to Bisley, then Birdlip, right to Cranham, then up another sharp hill before returning to Gloucester. We called this run our own Three Peaks Challenge!

Our next race was pencilled in for the Gloucester AC, which was the Two Bridges Race again in Scotland. A welcoming race with a bit of a holiday. During this time, we also had a chance to take in the Edinburgh Festival. Then take off up to Fort William for the gathering of the Highland Games and compete in the Ben Nevis Race in September. The weather is usually glorious. I recommend this activity holiday to anyone.

RACE 5

Next race on the agenda was our old favourite, the fourteenth running of the Two Bridges Race in Rosyth, Scotland, 29 August 1981.

Always starting in Dunfermline Glen over the Kincardine Bridge, finishing over the Forth Road Bridge in Rosyth Civil Service Sports Club.

The organisation of this race made this one of the best road races we have ever run in; a great weekend was had by all. Runners from all over the UK ran it. As a team, we always liked to try and beat the Scots in their own backyard (didn't always work out, though). For the past few years, we had also tried to beat Tipton Harriers AC (No 1. UK team at the time). We thought we had them in this race this particular year, but by Jove, they still beat us at our third year of racing them and only by one single point! (See results.)

Ah well, we licked our wounds; can always try again next year!

I must mention a new member to our Gloucester AC team, Les Davis, who only started running at 37 years of age. Within six years, he had won the world's age group cross-country championships, ran a sub 2hrs 20mins marathon and also won the London Marathon Veteran Championships! This ex-footballer and ex-rugby player only took up running to accompany his daughter in running training, which is remarkable! (More about Les later in the book.)

Shortly after this race, Gloucester AC were invited to a big relay race from Brest to Rennes in France, 267km spread over six individual legs.

The Two Bridges Race

29th AUGUST, 1981, KINCARDINE - FORTH

			h.	m.	s.
1.	M. Pickard	Epsom and Ewell H.	3	26	1
2.	C. Rutland	Banbury Harriers	3	34	33
3.	C. Woodward	Leamington C. and A.C.	3	39	16
4.	A. Richards	Tipton Harriers	3	41	21
5.	M. Daykin	Gloucester A.C.	3	42	3
6.	J. Watkins	South London Harriers	3	42	59
7.	F. S. Thomas	Chelmsford A.C.	3	43	46
8.	D. Dowdle	Gloucester A.C.	3	43	52
9.	G. Smith	Tipton Harriers	3	46	24
10.	D. Francis	Fife A.C.	3	46	38
11.	G. Kay	Stafford A.C.	3	46	45
12.	M. Ball	East Hull Harriers	3	48	18
13.	W. Humphreys	South London Harriers	3	49	3
14.	D. Attwell	Altrincham A.C.	3	49	37
15.	G. Hawkes	Leamington C. and A.C.	3	51	54
16.	E. Foley	Washington R.R.C. (U.S.A.)	3	53	1
17.	G. Armstrong	Lothian A.C.	3	53	43
18.	R. Stack	Washington R.R.C. (U.S.A.)	3	55	13
19.	E. Evason	Tipton Harriers	3	55	16
20.	L. Davis	Gloucester A.C.	3	57	13
21.	S. J. Bennett	Teviotdale Harriers	3	57	20
22.	G. Bennison	Bolton United Harriers	3	57	26

1. Tipton H., 32. 2. Gloucester A.C., 33. 3. S.L.H., 63. 4. Washington Running Club, 63. 5. Leamington A.C., 71. 6. Fife A.C., 72. 7. Bolton U.H., 78. Tipton H. '09. Pitreavie A.A.C., 155. Cambridge H., 224. Eighty-two finished.

38th position: Chris O'Carroll, Glos AC – 4.19.12

39th position: Ken Leyshon, Glos AC – 4.20.28

(Not our best results.)

53

Dave Dowdle
8th position

Gloucester
AC team, Les
Davis, who only
started running
at 37 years of
age

Sunday 19th Jan 1986

10 am start in Dunfermline Park. Cavin Woodward already clear of the rest.

FINISH

Finish at Rosyth Civil Service Club. Martin Daykin in 5th position

R A C E 6

Brest to Rennes Road Relay Race
Over 267 km (over 6 varying distance individual legs)
24 & 25 October 1981
29 August 1981

This race turned out to be one of the worst races we have ever run in!

Bad organisation!
No marshals!
Cheating going on, right from the start!

The race started in the early evening, through the night into the next morning. We all travelled over to Brest in three cars, ten of us in total. The team consisted of two cyclists (who had to accompany us the whole race, with our drinks), six runners, plus two extra drivers. The make-up of the team was as follows:

1st leg	Dave Price	JNR	17,900km
2nd leg	Chris O'Carroll	VET	47,530km
3rd leg	Les Davis	VET	43,200km
4th leg	Ken Leyshon	SNR	37,800km
5th leg	Martin Daykin	SNR	49,010km
6th leg	Joanne Davis	LADY	16,500km
7th member	Liz Daykin	Driver, Assistant / Glos AC	
8th member	Phil Hoddy	Driver, Assistant / Glos AC	
9th member	Brian Healey	Cyclist, Drinks / Severn Vale Racing Club	
7th member	Neil Jones	Cyclist, Drinks / Severn Vale Racing Club	

This race was sponsored by Martini.

Cyclists aid city runners in France

Over the weekend two members of the Severn Valley Cycle Racing Club, Brian Healey and Neal Jones, journeyed over to France to help Gloucester Athletics Club in the Brest-Rennes stage running race. Their job was to ride along by the Gloucester runners during the stages which ranged from 25 to 32 miles and support them by giving food, drink and during the night stages by lighting up the road. The team finished fourth overall

banque b de bretagne

6ᵉ TRANSARMORICAINE
24-25 OCTOBRE 1981
267 Km

SPIRIDON
❖
BRETAGNE

Brian Healey, Chris O'Carroll, Dave Price, Joanne Davis, Les Davis, Ken Leyshon, Martin Daykin, Neil Jones

BREST-RENNES

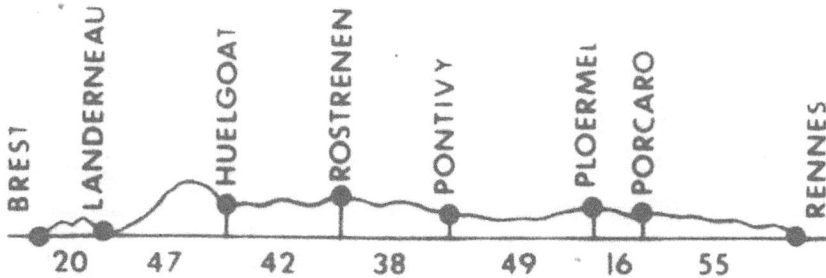

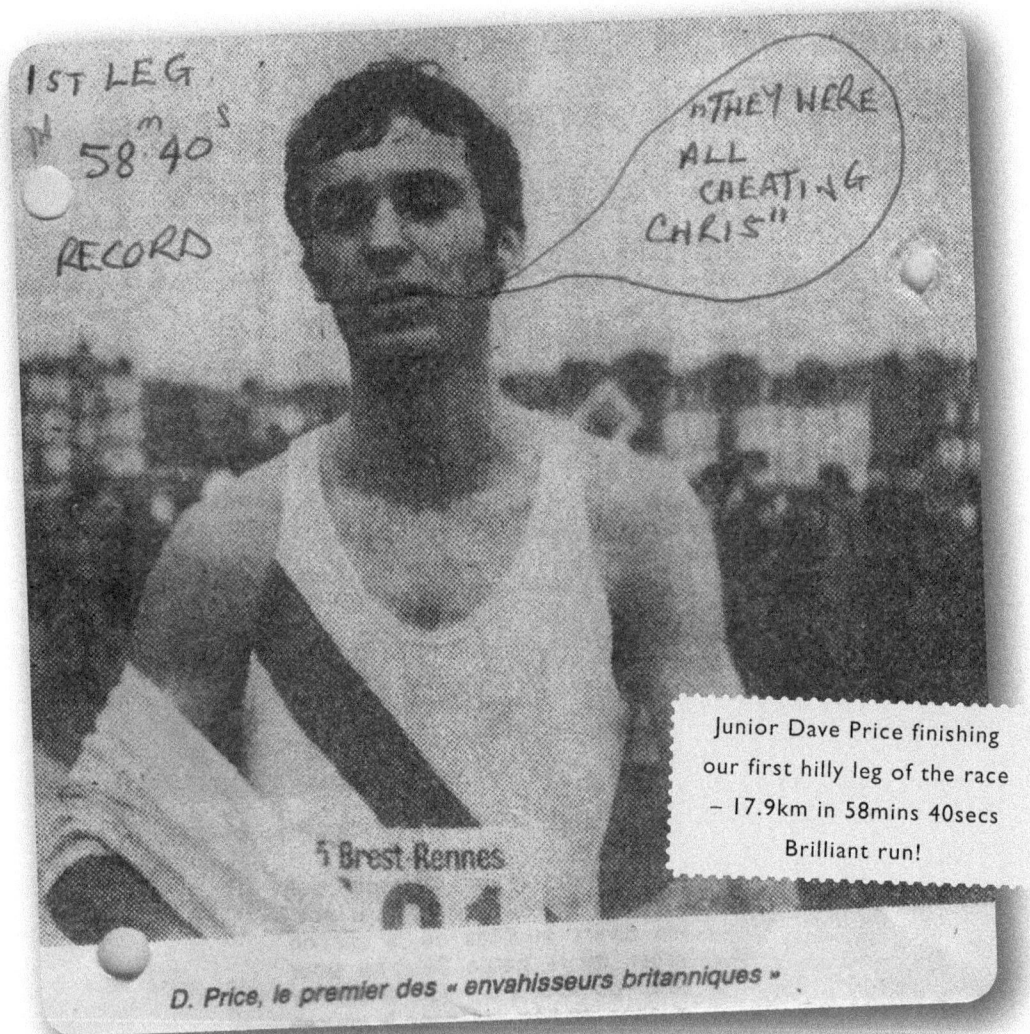

D. Price, le premier des « envahisseurs britanniques »

I mentioned in the preface about some skullduggery we encountered on our travels; well, this race was full of skullduggery, big-time cheating as we are about the find out!

⮑ LEG 1 — 17.9KM

Dave Price, a brilliant young junior runner for Gloucester AC, ran our first leg of 17.9km and finished in 1st place on a hilly course in 58 minutes and 04 seconds; however, he came in fuming, rushing in to hand over to me complaining in no uncertain terms, "They're cheating, Chris. Hanging onto car door handles going up hills." Young Neil, our cyclist, confirmed what Dave was saying. I replied that I would keep an eye out, so off I went on to Leg 2.

⮑ LEG 2 — 47.53KM

The race started early evening. On my run it was starting to get dark, but I had a 3-minute 26-second lead, so I got stuck in. Later, on a very hilly section towards the end of my run, a Frenchman rocketed by me with his cyclist aide. I mentioned to Neil, "He must be fit to be shifting like that after 40km covered." As we got to the top of the hill, both runner and cyclist had vanished, and we soon found out why! We could see his cyclist's rear light way in the distance, so it was obvious he had jumped on his mate's bike and hitched a lift down to the finish! Even more curiously, I actually finished 3rd, yet nobody else had passed me, so again the 1st or 2nd finisher, complete with his cyclist, had jumped in a car! It was blatantly obvious to us that there was no proper control in this race at all.

⮑ LEG 3 — 43.2KM

I handed over to Les and tried to warn him about the cheating that was going on as he set off into the night with Neil to do his third leg. Les seemed to be going okay with his run and didn't notice anything untoward, although some fast times were being recorded! Les completed his run in a good time, although the fastest man through looked suspicious. We were now back in 5th position. Les handed over to Ken on Leg 4.

61

⮑ LEG 4 — 37.8KM

Ken had also been warned about some cheating that was going on, but he still had a good run. The only thing he did notice was a rather fresh-looking runner jump out of a camper van and promptly vanish. Could this be the vehicle which also went past me earlier on the second leg? A van like that could definitely conceal a bike and a cyclist! We were now in 4th place and Ken handed over to Martin on the longest leg, when disaster struck. Earlier on, Phil, our driver, had indicated Martin was limping… he had pulled something warming up or stretching! It looked like he couldn't run. Phil even offered to take his place, but Martin said it should hold up and off he went on the longest leg.

⮑ LEG 5 — 49.1KM

We don't think Martin knew what was going on around him. Struggling to finish his leg to hand over to Joanne, he managed to still finish in a time of 3 hours 42 minutes and 55 seconds, which although way below his best, was very respectable considering the situation. The winner on his leg clocked 2 hours 45 minutes 55 seconds, a new world-record road run, by a vet no less! The 2nd man in also did a world-class time: 2 hours, 52 minutes and 25 seconds.

I think the first man had a faster car; it was just absolute cheating! We must remember that back then there were no chip timings, nobody marshalling throughout the night and all in all, the race was a complete shambles! By now, we had pretty much written this race off! Martin handed over to Joanne for the last leg. (Even if Martin had done his fastest world-class time, he wouldn't have beaten the first four teams to finish, who must have all been cheating to produce those times.)

⮑ LEG 6 — 16.5KM

Joanne finished the race for us. During her leg, she was feeling unwell and also struggled to finish, but considering she was sick en route, Joanne put in a courageous effort and we still finished in 4th position overall. Take out all the cheating, we definitely could have finished in the first three… we were, however, not quite finished with this race yet!

6ème BREST/RENNES en relais - 267 Kms -

les 24 et 25 octobre 1981

P A L M A R E S

1	G.S.I. PONTIVY	
2	SPIRIDON ILE DE FRANCE	16 H 10'02"
3	COUBRON	16H 33'W 29
4	GLOUCESTER A.C.	16H 51'12
5	EVREUX A.C.	17H 27'19
6	J.A. MELESSE	17H 32'06
7	C.A.S. INGUINIEL	17H 36'39
8	CHARTRES DE BRETAGNE	17H 43'53
9	ENTENTE DE LORIENT	17H 45'34
10	U.S. BAIN DE BRETAGNE	17H 48'50
11	C.S.K. LESNEVEN 1	17H 55'01
12	U.S. LIFFRE	18H 00'24
13	E.S.E.A.T. CESSON	18H 35'04
14	SPIRIDON LOUVAIN	18H 58'54
15	SAINT PABU	19H 23'48
16	C.A. GOELE	19H 24'53
17	A.S. TREGUEUX	19H 27'32
18		19H 30'38
19		
20		
21		
22		
23		
24		
25		

AFTER THE RACE (THAT'S WHEN THE FUN STARTED)

Martin, who spoke French quite fluently, spoke to several French teams about all the cheating that went on! One of the Brittany teams started an argument with a Parisian team who they knew had cheated. All of a sudden it got rather violent and out of control! (Bit like the race really.) Pushing and shoving with the odd punch thrown in, all while they were in front of the press. While all this chaos was happening around us, we knew that the race had been sponsored by Martini, who were kindly offering samples of their drinks to everyone in the presentation room. It didn't seem like the French were too bothered about that, so while the officials and organisers were still sorting everything out, we agreed that it seemed a shame to let all the drink go to waste, and we remarked, "Load up the car boots with the wine, liquor, brandy and cognac, lads."

"Are they still arguing? Yes, well, we better take the rest and get on the road back to Calais."

"Anyone coming back next year?" You must be bloody joking, cheating sods all of them, but what goes around comes back around, and it's safe to say we were all glad to see the back of this race! Still, it wasn't too bad a result really, finishing in 4th position.

Cheating sods all of them...

Our next race for the Gloucester AC Ultra Distance would be our biggest event yet! To put on a 24-hour track race in Gloucester City. Pencilled in for 23 May 1982, we had precisely seven months to organise it, train for it and race in it! Bring it on!

R A C E 7

Where do you start on this one, hey? A 24-hour track race in Gloucester, 6/7 months to sort it all out. Martin was the main organiser for the 100-mile road race previously, so it was only fair for myself to organise the 24-hour race. Just a few problems to sort out… crikey, what did I let myself in for? Got a 6-lane cinder track (440-yard lap), no cover, no lights, nothing at all (oh, and no money).

24 hour running event
CITY STAGES
TEST OF
ENDURANCE

WORLD record Jean Boussiquet is set to compete in a test of athletic endurance and courage in Gloucester in May.

Boussiquet will run in a 24 hour track race at the City Athletic Club's Blackbridge home. He can take part following the cancellation of a similar event in New York at about the same time.

The Frenchman holds the phenomenal record of running 169 miles and 705 yards and is probably the only runner to have run non-stop for 24 hours — a feat he achieved in Lausanne last year.

He has three times beaten the previous world mark of Tipton runner Ron Bentley and three weeks ago added over half-a-mile to the 24 hour record on the road at the Le Mans motor racing circuit to achieve 163

World's best in City race

GLOUCESTER Athletic Club's 24-hour track race will have one of the most powerful fields of World ranked ultradistance runners ever seen in one event.

The latest entries include Don Choi (California, USA) who is the World number one over 48 hours track running, Michel Meniour (France), world ranked over 100 kilometres, Joe Record (Australia), the world number two six day track runner and Mike Newton (London), who is World number one over six days, 200 kilometres and 200 miles.

World number one over 24 hours Jean Boussiquet (France) as revealed in the Citizen, entered the race some months ago.

And to add to the event a supreme test of courage and endurance, two women will be attempting to complete the 24 hours. No woman in Britain has ever completed this event.

Race organiser Chris O'Carroll said: "Word has got around the athletics world that Gloucester City's 24-hour track race is the one to be in.

"We are really looking forward to the event and are hoping that the Gloucester lads get in among them and really sort them out.

"This is their chance to prove that they can meet the World's best and take them on in one of the toughest sports there is," Mr. O'Carroll said.

So what do we need to make this happen?

1. Publicity (Gloucester squad now had lots of attention, so that wouldn't be too difficult)
2. Sponsors (Get the event in the media)
3. Club backing (Everyone totally behind us)
4. Officials (We need expertise for this one)
5. Volunteers (For lap recorders; no chips or computers in them days)
6. Refreshments (Helpers needed to look after runners for 24hrs+)
7. Entrants (6-lane track; how many can we look after?)
8. Prizes (Awards, but slight problem: no cash)
9. Printing (Programmes, signage, etc.)
10. Lighting (Around a cinder track in a field basically)
11. First aid (Definitely need cover for this one)

Well, looking at all that lot, I think we might need to hand this over to Terry Haines (of Glos AC). He's good at this sort of thing! Only kidding, I just have to get on with it, but I've got a good feeling about this race!

Soon enough, the word got around about this event and by a miracle it all began to fall into place! Firstly, Martin informed me that several overseas runners wanted to enter our event! This included runners from Canada, USA, Australia and France.

This definitely gave us the publicity that we wanted. Then great news, the current world record holder, Jean Gilles Boussiquet from France, was coming over to compete against us! We also got two of the UK's top ultra-distance ladies entering: Lynn Fitzgerald and Roz Paul, who had never run a race this long, it was all new to them... like us all! With UK entrants beginning to enter, our programme was taking shape.

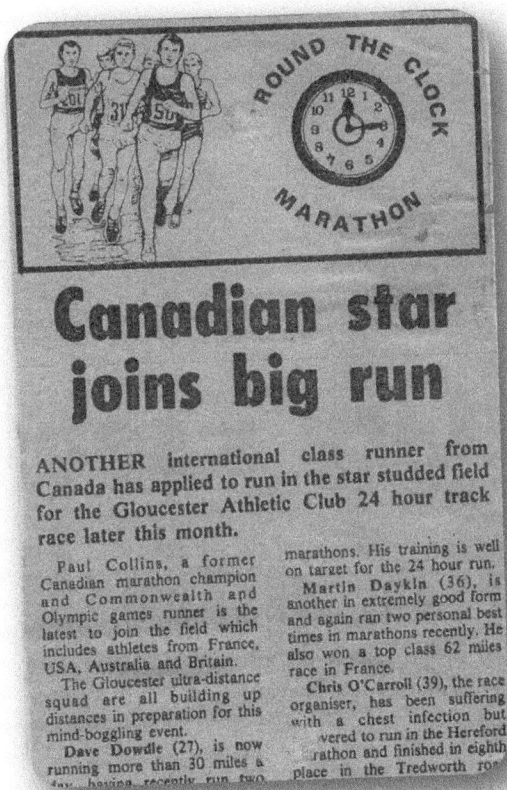

Canadian star joins big run

ANOTHER international class runner from Canada has applied to run in the star studded field for the Gloucester Athletic Club 24 hour track race later this month.

Paul Collins, a former Canadian marathon champion and Commonwealth and Olympic games runner is the latest to join the field which includes athletes from France, USA, Australia and Britain.

The Gloucester ultra-distance squad are all building up distances in preparation for this mind-boggling event.

Dave Dowdle (27), is now running more than 30 miles a day, having recently run two marathons. His training is well on target for the 24 hour run.

Martin Daykin (36), is another in extremely good form and again ran two personal best times in marathons recently. He also won a top class 62 miles race in France.

Chris O'Carroll (39), the race organiser, has been suffering with a chest infection but ʳecovered to run in the Hereford ᵐarathon and finished in eighth place in the Tredworth roᵃ

67

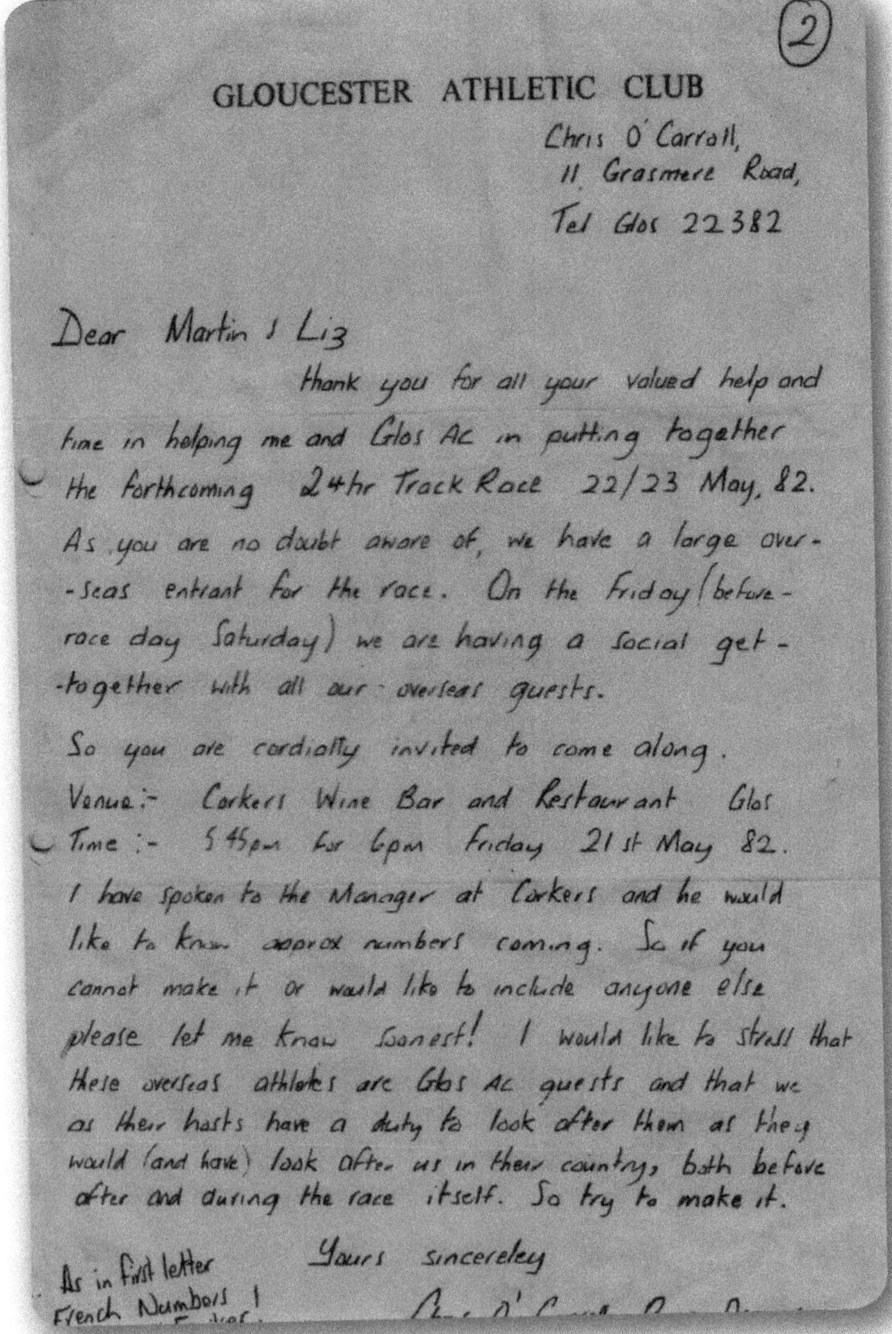

②

GLOUCESTER ATHLETIC CLUB

Chris O'Carrall,
11 Grasmere Road,
Tel Glos 22382

Dear Martin & Liz

thank you for all your valued help and
time in helping me and Glos Ac in putting together
the forthcoming 24hr Track Race 22/23 May. 82.
As you are no doubt aware of, we have a large over-
-seas entrant for the race. On the Friday (before-
race day Saturday) we are having a Social get-
-together with all our overseas guests.

So you are cordially invited to come along.
Venue :- Corkers Wine Bar and Restaurant   Glos
Time :- 5 45pm for 6pm Friday 21 st May 82.
I have spoken to the Manager at Corkers and he would
like to know approx numbers coming. So if you
cannot make it or would like to include anyone else
please let me know Soonest! I would like to stress that
these overseas athletes are Glos Ac guests and that we
as their hosts have a duty to look after them as they
would (and have) look after us in their country, both before
after and during the race itself. So try to make it.

Yours sincereley

As in first letter
French Numbers !

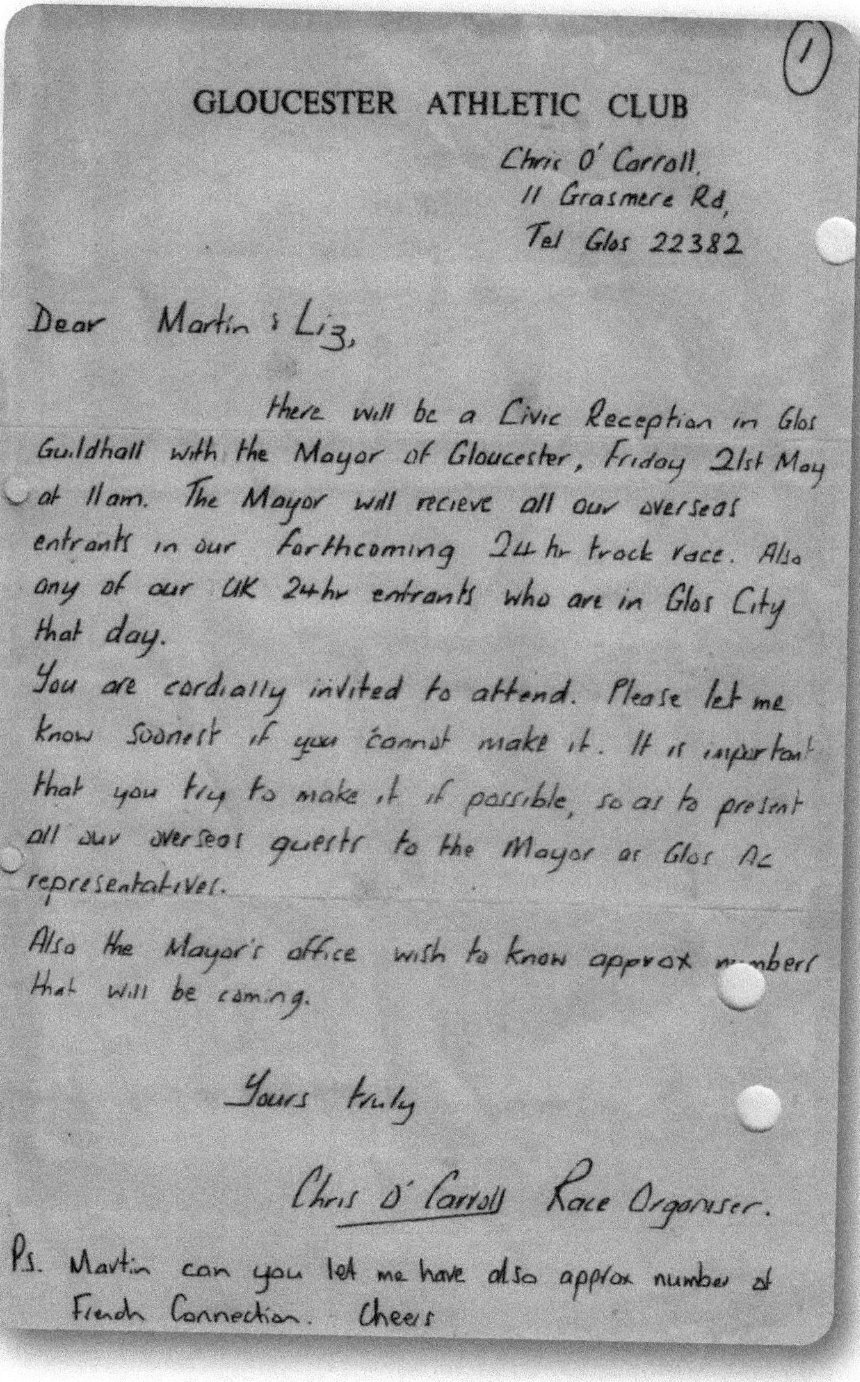

①

GLOUCESTER ATHLETIC CLUB

Chris O'Carroll.
11 Grasmere Rd,
Tel Glos 22382

Dear Martin & Liz,

there will be a Civic Reception in Glos
Guildhall with the Mayor of Gloucester, Friday 21st May
at 11am. The Mayor will recieve all our overseas
entrants in our forthcoming 24 hr track race. Also
any of our UK 24hr entrants who are in Glos City
that day.

You are cordially invited to attend. Please let me
know soonest if you cannot make it. It is important
that you try to make it if possible, so as to present
all our overseas guests to the Mayor as Glos Ac
representatives.

Also the Mayor's office wish to know approx numbers
that will be coming.

Yours truly

Chris O'Carroll Race Organiser.

P.s. Martin can you let me have also approx number of
French Connection. Cheers

1. Publicity (Was gaining ground in local/national media)
2. Sponsors (Finally coming forward with help)
3. Club backing (Glos AC organising tents, etc.)
4. Officials (The RRC of UK were coming to help, Grade 1 timekeepers of this)
5. Volunteers (Lap recorders Arthur and Sheila Daley took charge of this)
6. Refreshments (Glos AC were already sorting out who would do what)
7. Entrants (Total of twenty-six entrants so far; this was manageable)
8. Prizes (Due to sponsors, everyone will get an award)
9. Printing (Martin's mum and dad ran a printing firm… very handy)
10. Lighting (Local hire firm, Ermin Plant Hire, supplied the men and lighting for free)
11. First aid (St John Ambulance and my wife, Bernie O'Carroll, who was a trained nurse)

So everything was falling into place and people involved in the event were beavering away. The Gloucester Ultra-Distance Squad were also starting to pile on the intense training.

When we trained, we ran shorter runs at 6mins miling or faster and 6/7mins miling on longer runs, mainly on hilly terrain. For this race, we had a good six months to get stronger and fitter. As the months progressed, with 2/3 weeks to go, it was time to come off the hills, ease down on the mileage and prepare for the race itself. (Plus, it was a relief not to have a shower two to three times a day.) By the time race day comes along, we will all be champing at the bit to get running on an easy, flat surface.

Meanwhile, on the organisational front, and now nearing the race start date, there were problems starting to arise. When we raced abroad, the race organisers always got accommodation for us with local families; however, we had just been informed that the French were coming en masse with Boussiquet. The RRC senior committee were up from London, plus lots of other entrants from the UK and abroad who would be arriving at different times on different days! Who would be the organiser of all this then? Well, we just had to get straight on to it and get it sorted out!

Knowing the French like a bit of pomp and splendour, we quickly arranged a civic reception for them, with the mayor of Gloucester and various dignitaries on the Friday before the race, at the Guildhall. Also arranged on the Friday night was a big evening meal and a big get-together with everyone from the UK and abroad (who were here already), in Corkers restaurant in Gloucester, with a meal of their choice. The chefs did us proud! I think the French contingents were very impressed and happy. Boussiquet and his party all came from the La Rochelle area of France.

Another problem which we had to sort out was getting everyone fixed for a bed and place to sleep that Friday night before the race day on the Saturday. My next door neighbours Brian and Lindy Wood got John Jewell, president of the RRC and Mark Pickard of Epsom and Ewell to stay overnight. Martin and Liz Daykin luckily managed to sort accommodation out for all the French runners and teams. Some of the runners had decided to bring their own tents to the race venue, and other runners from the UK arrived on the Saturday morning before the 10 am start time.

Civic reception – for Gloucester AC Squad,
prior to their 24-hour track race in Glos

So everyone was sorted, except we had a problem in that two French gentlemen were still without any sleeping arrangements that Friday evening! I drove to the nearest pub, the Double Gloucester in Longlevens, and made an urgent request at the bar. "Has anyone got a spare room for these two French gentlemen?" A certain man, Mr Dave Hodges, and his good wife, Liz, said that they would look after them and sort them out for the night. So we drove with them to their house in Longlevens to see that everything was okay, and arranged to pick them up early Saturday morning. Dave and Liz kindly gave them supper and a big breakfast, so I'm told! Fellow kindred spirits!

So that was finally everyone sorted out.

⮑ SATURDAY AM – RACE DAY

Pick up the two gentlemen from Dave and Liz Hodges and then straight up to the Gloucester track to prepare for the 10 am race start. Official programme was available to purchase (35p, bit expensive) and everyone was there. Twenty-six entrants in total, but on the day there were nineteen that showed up and started.

Marquee tents up, lighting in place, runners' tented village inside of the track ready, and official lap recorders all there. Everything was in place, so I was good to go to get ready for the 24-hour race.

Nineteen entrants out of twenty-six finally toed the line to start at 10 am. We started 10 minutes late, but with great relief, we were off and the race began.

Gloucester A.C. Club extend a warm welcome to all runners and officials alike to our 24hr. Track Race Promotion 22nd/23rd May, 1982, both from overseas and here in U.K.

Hope everything works out well for you and it will be a race to remember. So only remains for me to say

Bon Voyage and Good Luck to You All From All at Glos. A.C.

Signed

C O' Carroll

Chris O'Carroll,
Race Organiser.

24-Hour Race Entrants			
1	Jean Gilles Boussiquet	St Pierre D'Amilly	France World Best 24hr
2	Don Choi	California	US World No. 2 48hr Road
3	Joe Record	Australia	World No. 2 6 Day Track
4	Paul Collins	Highgate Harriers	Canadian World Ranked 24hr
5	Martin Daykin	Gloucester AC	UK World Ranked 100k 100mls
6	Dave Dowdle	Gloucester AC	UK World Ranked 100k 100mls
7	Chris O'Carroll	Gloucester AC	UK World Ranked 100k 100mls
8	Ken Leyshon	Gloucester AC	UK World Ranked 100k 100mls
9	John Towers	East Hull Harriers	UK World Ranked 100mls 24hr
10	Bruce Slade	Exeter Harriers	UK World Ranked 100mls 24hr
11	Malcolm Campbell	Notts AC	UK World Ranked VET 100mls 24hr
12	Bromley Clarke	Berryhill AC	UK Ultra Runner
13	Bob Holmes	Notts AC	UK Ultra Runner 24hr
14	Ken Shaw	Cambridge Harriers	UK Ultra Runner 100k 100mls 24hr
15	Mark Pickard	Epsom and Ewell	UK World Ranked 100k, 100mls, 24hr (British Record-Holder 24hr)
16	Richard Thornton	Salisbury AC	UK Ultra 24hr Runner
17	Herb Groom		USA Marathon Runner
18	Lynn Fitzgerald	Highgate Harriers	UK Marathon Ultra Runner
19	Roz Paul	Barnet AC	UK Marathon Ultra Runner

The Gloucester runners in tomorrow's gruelling race. From the left, Martin Daykin, Dave Dowdle, Ken Leyshon and Chris O'Carroll.

READY FOR THE OFF!

GLOUCESTER'S reputation for producing some of the best ultra-distance runners in the world has attracted the strongest field ever seen for one of the most gruelling events — the 24 hour track race which starts tomorrow.

At 10.00 am, a field packed with record holders and world ranked performers at several astonishing distances and races, will start out on one of the athletic world's pinnacles of effort and achievement.

Leading the top-class runners will be Frenchman Jean Boussiquet — the world's best over 24 hours on the track and the road.

Boussiquet has run 164 miles on the track, but race organiser Chris O'Carroll said this record could go.

"One hundred and 70 miles is feasible and the Gloucester lads are dying to have a go. We are all well known on the continent where this sport is very big and this has resulted in such a strong field," he said.

Strongest challenge

Runners are coming from as far away as America and Australia as well as the top Britons, to run in the Gloucester event, but Chris said the strongest challenge could come from the crack Gloucester ultra-distance squad of Martin Daykin, Dave Dowdle, Ken Leyshon and himself.

"We have a great tradition with some of the best training grounds in the world in the local hills. In the 100 miles event, you look at the world rankings and see four from Gloucester in the top 50 with two right at the top."

The race has taken months of organisation and during the 24 hours, a back-up team providing food and drink for the competitors is vital.

Runners will be taking liquid every 15 minutes and it has been estimated that during the course of the event, an athlete's intake will be an incredible five gallons.

"Most of the runners will stop for meals, a rest and to change clothes and shoes during the night. But Boussiquet just sets up a reclining chair by the side of the track and never changes during the course of the race."

Unique event

"It is going to be a very close run thing and we want as many people as possible to come down and watch this unique event. Food and refreshment is available throughout the night," Chris added.

Two women from London are in the field and they are confidently expected to break the United Kingdom record.

For the 27 competitors this event is something special, one which even extremely fit athletes would find far too daunting. Only a select band are confident enough to contemplate running such distances.

Chris O'Carroll summed up the race's appeal: "It is the athletics equivalent of climbing Everest."

The effort begins at the City Athletic Club's Blackbridge headquarters at 10.00 am. The race ends on Sunday morning.

CITIZEN 21.5.82

GLOUCESTER
ATHLETIC
CLUB

24 hour
RACE

Blackbridge track
22nd/23rd May 1982

Sat 10a.m. start
Sun 10a.m. finish

OFFICIAL PROGRAMME 35p

RACE OFFICIALS

Race Organiser	Chris O'Carroll	Gloucester AC
Chief Timekeeper	Don Turner Grade 1	Epsom & Ewell AC
Ass. Timekeeper	Cliff Franks Grade 1	Cheltenham Harriers
Ass. Timekeeper	Arthur Birt Grade II	Gloucester AC
Ass. Timekeeper	Bob Hussey Grade III	Gloucester AC
Chief Laprecorder	Arthur Daley	Gloucester AC
Ass. Chief Laprecorder	Sheila Daley	Gloucester AC
Chief Referee	Mick Price	Gloucester AC
Chief Co-ordinator Race Day	Terry Haines	Gloucester AC
Chief First Aid	Mr. Gracie	St. Johns Ambulance

Prize Giving Approx. 11 a.m. Sunday 23rd

Refreshments served throughout the event.   A hot meal will be available in the evening of 22nd at a nominal charge.

SPECIAL ACKNOWLEDGEMENT AND THANKS TO

Birds Eye Walls Limited	Walton on Thames
Ermin Plant Hire Limited	Gloucester
Stroud Building Society	Stroud
Whitbread Brewery Limited	Cheltenham
Nike International Limited	Durham
Beecham Foods Limited	Middlesex
Tip Top Confections Limited	Gloucester
Wally International CB Club	Matson
Exclusive 60 CB Club	Churchdown
Pirates Heroes CB Breakers Club	Gloucester
Scoo B Doo Special Baby Unit Royal Hosp.	Gloucester
Gloucester Leisure Centre	Gloucester
Limbless Ex Service Club Glos. Branch	Stroud
St. John Ambulance Brigade	Gloucester
Mike Price Gloucester A.C.	Gloucester
Terry Haines Gloucester Ath. Club	Gloucester
Arthur and Sheila Daley Glos. A.C.	Gloucester
Don Turner RRC Gt. Britain	London
Dave Palmer Exclusive 60 Club	Churchdown
FM Breakers Society CB Club	Gloucester

AND TO ANYONE ELSE NOT MENTIONED ABOVE

THANK YOU ALL FOR YOUR ASSISTANCE IN HELPING

GLOS ATHLETIC CLUB IN THIS PROMOTION

Race Organiser

Chris O'Carroll

Also like to thank Mr. Eaton and his Groundsman Staff for their valued help.

LISTS OF ENTRANTS

Number	Name	Club	Country
1.	Jean Gilles Boussiquet	St. Pierre D'Amilly	France
2.	Don Choi	California	U.S.A.
3.	Joe Record		Australia
4.	Paul Collins	Highgate Harriers	Canada
5.	Mike Newton	South London Harriers	U.K.
6.	Martin Daykin	Gloucester A.C.	U.K.
7.	Dave Dowdle	Gloucester A.C.	U.K.
8.	Chris O'Carroll	Gloucester A.C.	U.K.
9.	Ken Leyshon	Gloucester A.C.	U.K.
10.	Alec Randall	South London Harriers	U.K.
11.	John Towers	East Hull Harriers	U.K.
12.	Bruce Slade	Exeter Harriers	U.K.
13.	Malcolm Cambell	Notts. A.C.	U.K.

LIST OF ENTRANTS

Number	Name	Club	Country
14.	Bromley Clarke	Berryhill A.C.	U.K.
15.	Bob Holmes	Notts. A.C.	U.K.
16.	Ken Shaw	Cambridge Harriers	U.K.
17.	Mark Guichard	Dartford Harriers	U.K.
18.	Stephen Carley	Cheltenham Harriers	U.K.
19.	Brian Heaford	Cheltenham Harriers	U.K.
20.	Bob Hamilton	Cheltenham Harriers	U.K.
21.	Richard Thornton	Salisbury A.C.	U.K.
22.	David Haywood	Bristol A.C.	U.K.
23.	Henri Girault		France
24.	Lynn Fitzgerald (lady)	Highgate Harriers	U.K.
25.	Roz Paul (lady)		U.K.
26.	Herb Groom		U.S.A.

Brief Past History of Entrants in Glos. 24 hr Race

1. World Best Performance at 24 hr track Dist. 164 miles
World Best Performance at 24 hr road Dist. 161 miles

2. World No. 2 performer at 48 hour road
World Ranked 24 hour 6 day track

3. World No. 2 performer at 6 day track
World ranked 24 hour and 24 hour track performer

4. World ranked 24 hour runner, ex Canadian marathon champ
Ex Commonwealth, Olympic marathon runner

5. World best performer at 200 mile, 200 km, 48 hour, and
6 day track - on every ultra dist. world ranking list.

6. World Ranked No, 1 100 mile 1981 English record holder 100 mile
World Ranked No. 2 100 km. 1981

7. World Ranked No. 2 100 mile 1981 7th London to Brighton 1981
English 2nd Ranked 100 miles   100 km time 7hrs 1 min 1980

8. World Ranked No 33 100 mile road 1981
Best Marathon 2hr. 27 mins. Best 100 km time 7hrs. 59 mins

9. World Ranked 100 mile road runner
London to Brighton Winning team member 1979

10. 24 hr. track race Best distance 95 miles 1979
London to Brighton 7hrs. 2 mins marathon 2.47 veteran

11. World ranked 100 mile 24 hour, 48 hour and 6 day track
runner 1981, 1982

12. Joint World Record holder 24 hr track relay 1982
Successful 24 hour track race runner

13. Joint World record holder 24 hr. track relay 1982
World ranked 24 hr. track race runner 139 miles

Brief Past History of Entrants in Glos. 24 hr. Race

Joint World record holder 24 hour relay
24 hour track race runner

14.

Successful 24 hour track race runner
London to Brighton 6 hours

15.

Successful 24 hour track race runner 129 miles
Veteran of over 100 marathons Competed in several Lond. to Brighton

16.

Marathon Runner   Newcomer to this event

17.

Marathon Runner   Newcomer to this event

18.

Marathon Runner   Newcomer to this event

19.

Marathon Runner   Newcomer to this event

20.

Marathon & ultra dist. runner   Newcomer to this event

21.

Successfully completed 2 24hr. road and track races
Also a 6 day event man

22.

Unknown quantity marathon/ultra dist. runner

23.

Marathon/Ultra distance runner   Newcomer to this event
Winner London to Brighton Race & Glos 18   ladies races

24.

Marathon/Ultra dist. runner, 2nd London to Brighton 1981
Downsman 100 mile in 22hours.   Newcomer to this event

25.

Marathon distance runner/unknown quantity

26.

24 Hour Alltime List as at 13th October 1981

(Andy Milroy)

miles	yards	Kms			
169	705	272.624	Jean-Gilles Boussiquet (France)	2/3.5.81	Lausanne
164	192	264.108	Boussiquet (2)	11/12.10.80	Blackburn
163	1249	263.466	Mark Pickard (Epsom & Ewell H)	10/11.10.81	Barnet
162	537	261.204 +	Park Barner (USA)	1/2.6.79	Huntington Ch
162	229	260.925 +	Boussiquet (3)	19/20.4.80	Coetquidan
161	545	259.603	Ron Bentley (Tipton H)	3/4.11.73	Walton
159	562	256.400	Wally Hayward (South Africa)	20/21.11.53	Motspur Park
158	1622	255.760	Mike Newton (South London H)	10/11.10.81	Barnet
156	791	251.701	Newton (2)	2/3.5.81	Lausanne
156	439	251.459	Tom Roden (South London H)	15/16.10.77	Crystal Palace
154	1335	249.060	Dave Goodwin (Thetford AC)	10/11.10.81	Barnet
154	1226	248.960	Derek Reynolds (Blackheath H)	20/21.11.53	Motspur Park
154	1181	248.918 +	Adriano Piccinali (Italy)	27.11.77	Bergamo
154	791	248.563	Newton (3)	11/12.10.80	Blackburn
154	421	248.224	Alain Cornioley (Switzerland)	2/3.5.81	Lausanne
154	414	248.218 +	Patrick Lavasseur (France)	31.3.79	Coetquidan
153	1143	247.275	Dave Jones (Blackburn H)	27/28.10.79	Crystal Palace
152	1599	246.082 +	Barner (2)	27/28.10.78	New Jersey
152	794	245.347 +	Bretislav Molata (Czechoslovakia)	16.9.77	Ostrava
150	1455	242.733 +	Alexis Martinet (France)	17.6.78	Ulis
150	1447	242.725	Pickard (2)	11/12.10.80	Blackburn
150	1064	242.374 +	Rino Lavelli (Italy)	24.10.76	Bergamo
146	675	235.600	Dave Cooper (Cambridge H)	10/11.10.81	Barnet
145	1314	234.557	Derek Funnell (Epsom & Ewell H)	15/16.10.77	Crystal Palace
145	408	233.729	Bob Van Deusen (USA)	2/3.8.80	Portland, Ore
144	1744	233.341	Gerard Stenger (France)	11/12.10.80	Blackburn
142	1614	230.003	Joe Record (Australia)	27/28.10.79	Crystal Place
141	1509	228.298	Vaclav Kamenik (Czechoslovakia)	2/3.5.81	Lausanne
141	863	227.707	Robin Stamper (South Africa)	26/27.7.74	Durban
140	1351	226.554 +	Carmelo Andreatta (Italy)	21.10.74	Trento
140	1219	226.423	Graham Peddie (Epsom & Ewell H)	27/28.10.79	Crystal Palace
140	716	225.963	Gerald Rosset (Switzerland)	2/3.5.81	Lausanne
140	100	225.400 +	Josef Grossmann (Czechoslovakia)	16.9.77	Ostrava
139	852	224.470	Charlie Hunn (South London H)	10/11.10.81	Barnet
139	461	221.121 +	Claudio Storpin (Italy)	27.9.74	Milan

Female 24 Hours

126m 749y/203.462k	Sue Medaglia(US)	26/27.9.81 Greenwich,Conn.
123m 593y/198.491k	Sue Ellen Trapp(US)	29.2/1.3.80 Miami
116m 676y/187.302k(i)	Sue Kahler(US)	21.11.81 Auburn,New York
116m 269y/186.930k	Edith Couhe(Fr)	16/17.5.81 Coetquidan
113m1183y/182.936k(I)	Marcy Schwam(US)	17/18.8.79 Woodside,Calif
106m 236y/171.263k	Mavis Hutchison(SA)	27/28.8.71 Johannesburg
105m1717y/170.551k	Lydi Pallares(US)	6.6.81 Coventry,R.I.
104m1561y/168.800k(2)	Ann Sayer(Essex Ladies)	10/11.4.82 Nottingham

(i) Indoors. (I) Marcy has reportedly improved on the world best
recently, no details as yet. (2) This distance achieved on route
to 182m1326y in 48 hours. Has achieved 118.5 miles/190.7k on
the road in 24 Hours - 4/5.5.80 Torcy, France.

Gloucester A.C. Club extend a warm welcome to all
runners and officials alike to our 24hr. Track Race
Promotion 22nd/23rd May, 1982, both from overseas
and here in U.K.

Hope everything works out well for you and it will
be a race to remember.   So only remains for me to
say

Bon Voyage and Good Luck to
You All From All at Glos. A.C.

Signed

C O'Carroll

Chris O'Carroll,
Race Organiser.

The race was also to raise money for Scoo-B-Doo, a special baby unit at Gloucester Royal Hospital, and for the Gloucester Athletic Club's track appeal fund. (From a cinder track to an all-weather track.) This was through programme sales and donations.

Quiet start to 24-hour race at Glos AC cinder track (nineteen entrants) 10 am start time

Arthur Daley of Gloucester AC – chief lap recorder Preparing for the start of the 24-hour track race in Glos, 1982

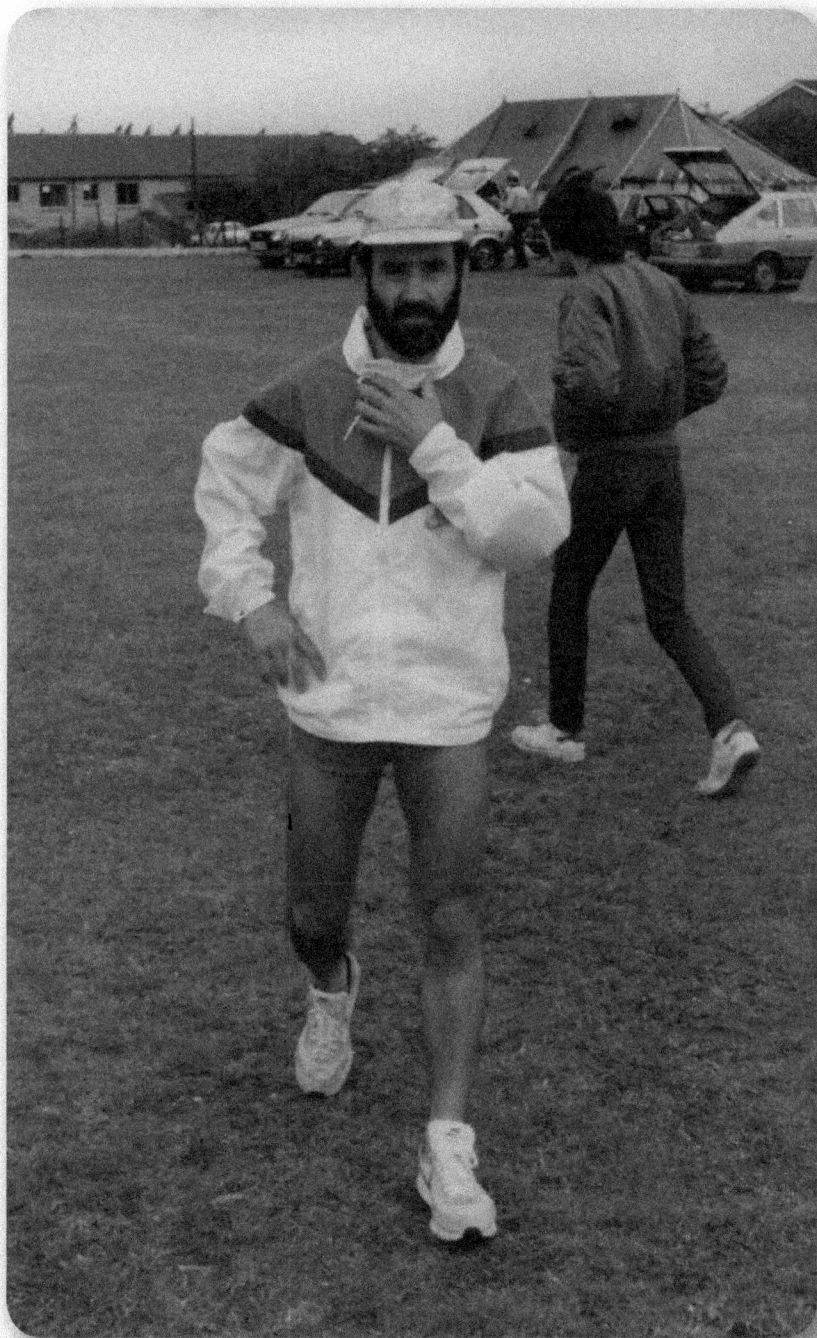

World record holder
170 miles+ Jean

Martin shaking hands with Don Choi from
the USA – everyone assembling on the track

Chris O'Carroll having a last look as organiser before
the off! Ken and Dave of Glos AC on the front grid!

Arthur Daley laying down some instructions

Finally ready for the off, 10.10 am

Would this be another Glos AC Ultra Squad event? Or would the formidable opposition blow us away? Right from the gun, Mark Pickard made his move into the lead. At 10 miles, he was still ahead. He reached the 30-mile mark in 3hrs 40mins 42secs, followed by the Gloucester pair, Martin in 2nd and Dowdle in 3rd, 7mins behind, but early days! Chris in 11th position with Ken in 10th at the 30-mile mark. By 40 miles, everyone was still in the same positions, but Chris now moved up to 7th position in 5hrs 20mins 02secs.

The ladies were also running well, with Lynn at 40 miles in 8th position, 5hrs 21mins 41secs. Roz Paul in 11th position at 40 miles in a time of 5hrs 36mins 51secs, 15 minutes behind Lynn.

So four Gloucester runners in the top ten, not bad, but still early days!

Boussiquet was not doing too well; he went through 40 miles in 5th place with a time of 5hrs 13mins 27secs, and by 50 miles, he had dropped to 12th with a time of 7hrs

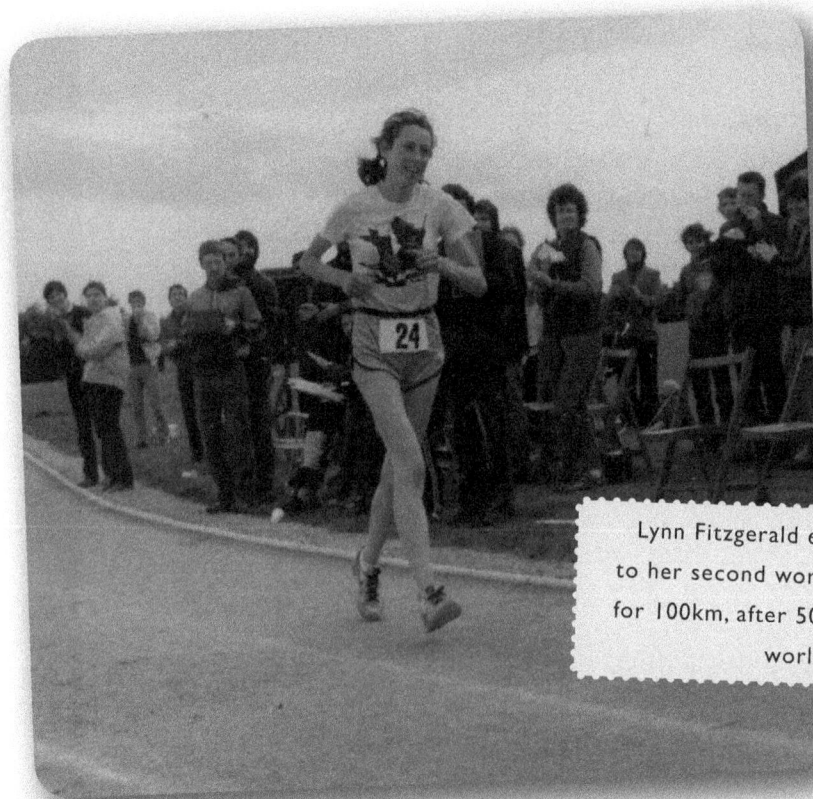

Lynn Fitzgerald en route to her second world best for 100km, after 50 miles, world best!

35mins 35secs. The race unfortunately ended for him at 60 miles when he called it a day in 10th position in a time of 9hrs 11mins 35secs.

Likewise, D. Choi started opening at the 10-mile mark in 3rd place, before dropping slowly back to 17th place at 60 miles before he also retired from the race.

Herb Groom was also struggling earlier on and he retired at the 70-mile mark in 17th position.

By the 80-mile mark, sixteen runners were left, still four Gloucester runners and both ladies battling it out. Martin by 80 miles had taken the lead in 10hrs 06mins 02secs. Both Mark and Dave knew he was going for the 200km world record and were both watching each other, with Mark leading Dave by 12mins at the 80-mile mark. Lynn was still in 1st, running very strong. 12hrs 11mins 16secs in 6th position overall and a 27mins lead over Roz. Chris and Ken were in 4th and 7th position at 80 miles. Johnny Tower (Hull City) was running well in 5th position, 11hrs 19mins 30secs. Already, everyone had been running in the darkness of the night, now getting colder and it was raining.

While I was still running, we heard that Lynn had already broken two world records (lady) for 50 miles in 6hrs 41mins 58secs. Then her second world record for the 100km mark in a time of 8hrs 39mins 10secs. By the 100-mile mark, Martin was getting stronger and faster, coming in at a time of 12hrs 52mins 10secs. Mark Pickard had a time of 13hrs 10mins 43secs. Dave Dowdle, 13hrs 31mins 29secs, Chris now 4th, 14hrs 19mins 10secs, and Ken Leyshon in 7th, 16hrs 01min 18secs. Before this, Lynn was struggling and was off world record pace at 100 miles and missed a world record, but she still set the British best with a time of 15hrs 58mins 15secs. The world best was by Marey Scharm of the USA in 15hrs 44mins 27secs.

Martin *en route* to his world record 200km

Roz taking advice from
one of the famous Bently
brothers of Tipton Harriers.

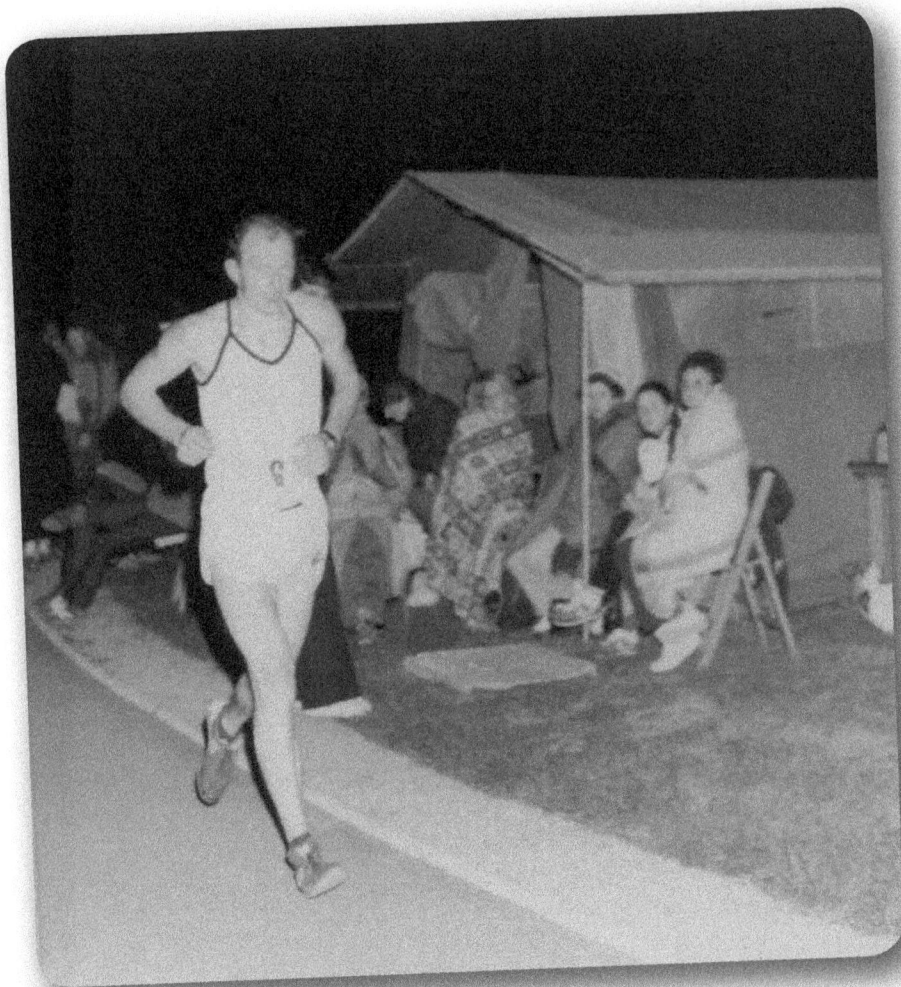

Martin Daykin going past
keen spectators, wrapped
up for the night

Malcolm Campbell,
Notts AC

Lynn being cheered on by spectators, going through to her fifth world best for 24hr after 150km and 200km world bests!

Bob Holmes Notts AC - also
getting nearer the finishing time

Ken Shaw braving it out in the rainstorm!

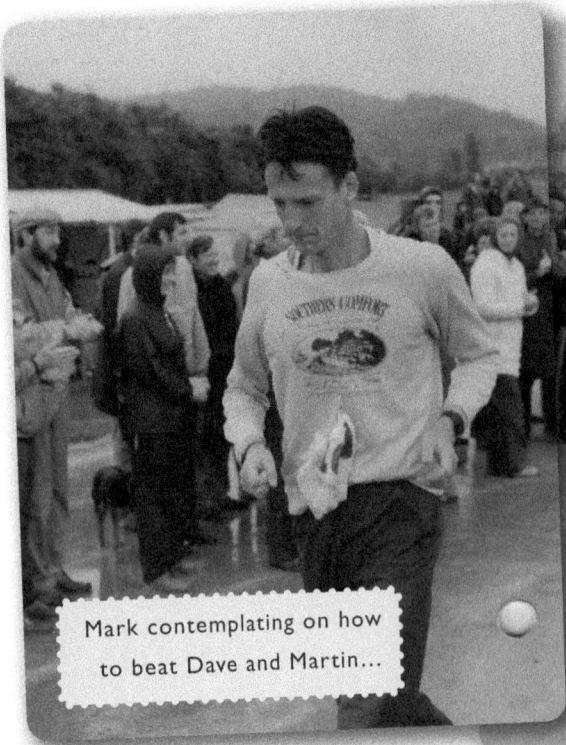

Bob Holmes, Notts AC, also sticking it out in the rain!

Bruce Slade, Exeter Harriers

Mark contemplating on how to beat Dave and Martin...

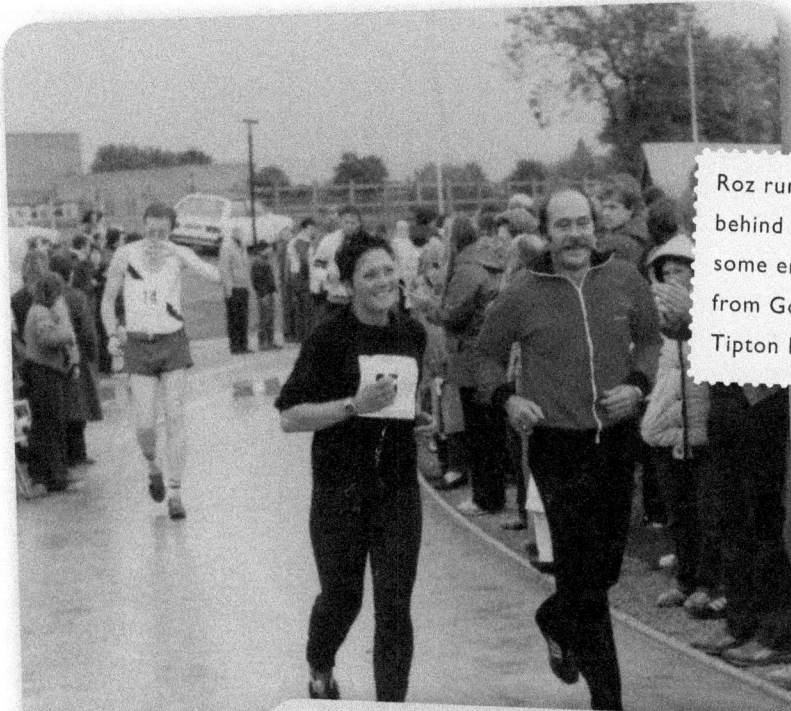

Roz running well behind Lynn with some encouragement from Gordon Bently - Tipton Harriers

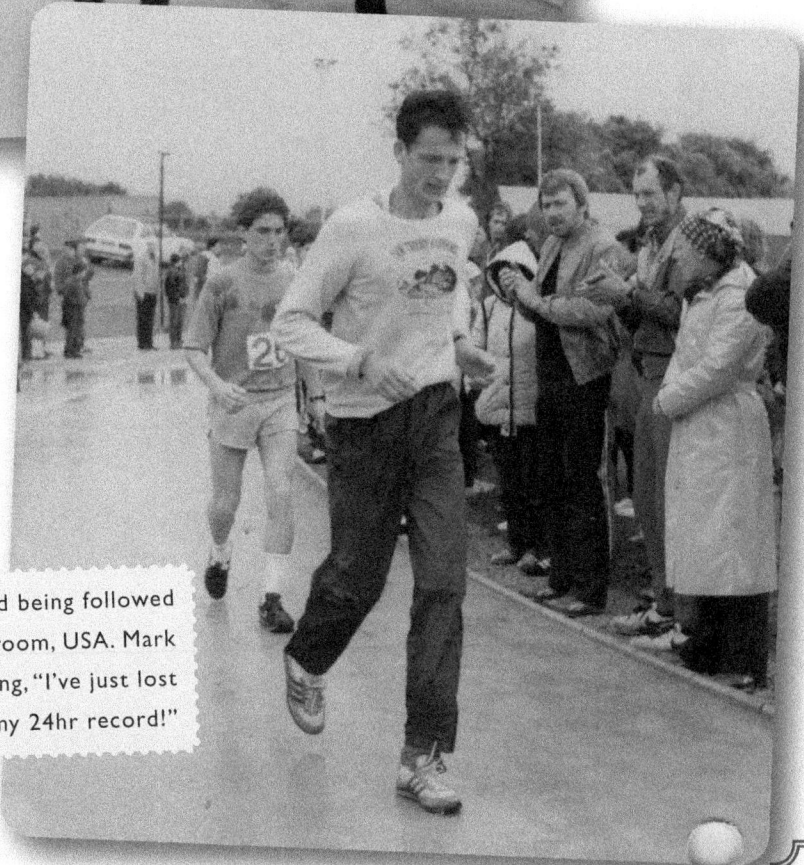

Mark Pickard being followed by Herb Groom, USA. Mark contemplating, "I've just lost my 24hr record!"

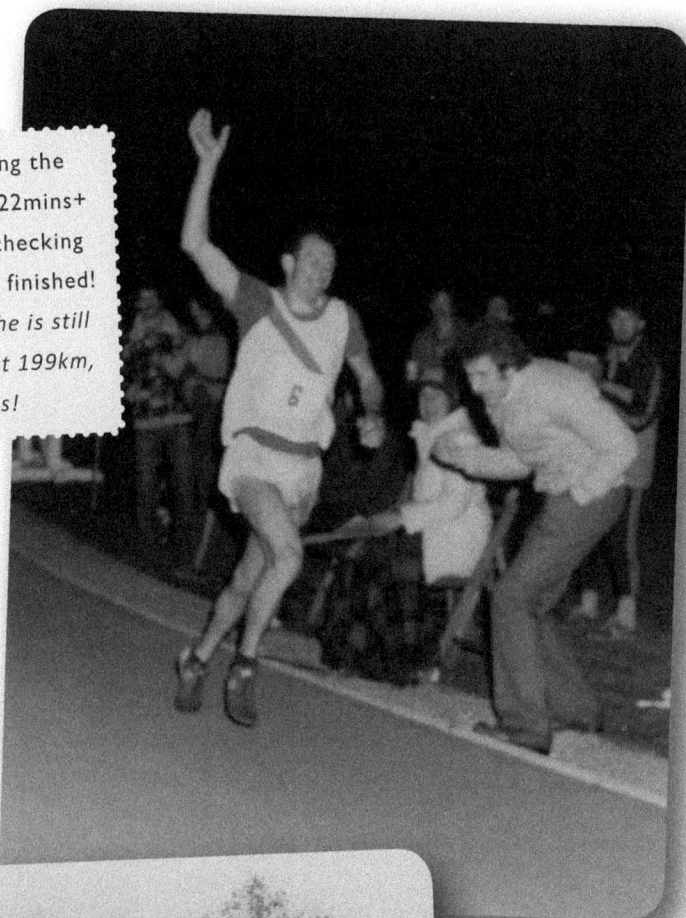

Martin Daykin smashing the 200km world record by 22mins+ alas 400m short after checking lap recorders after race finished! To all of us at Glos AC, he is still a world record holder at 199km, 600m in our eyes!

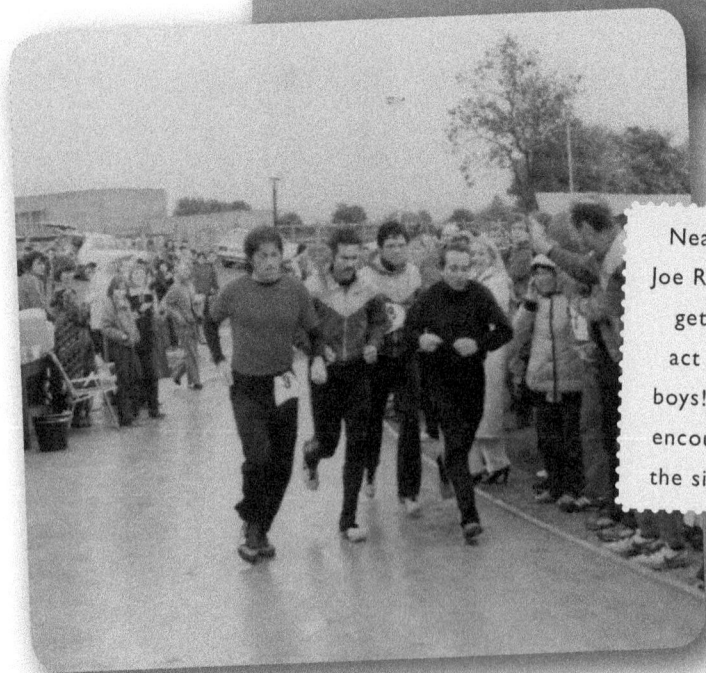

Nearing the finish. Joe Record, Australia, getting in on the act with the Glos boys! Martin and Liz encouraging Dave at the side of the track

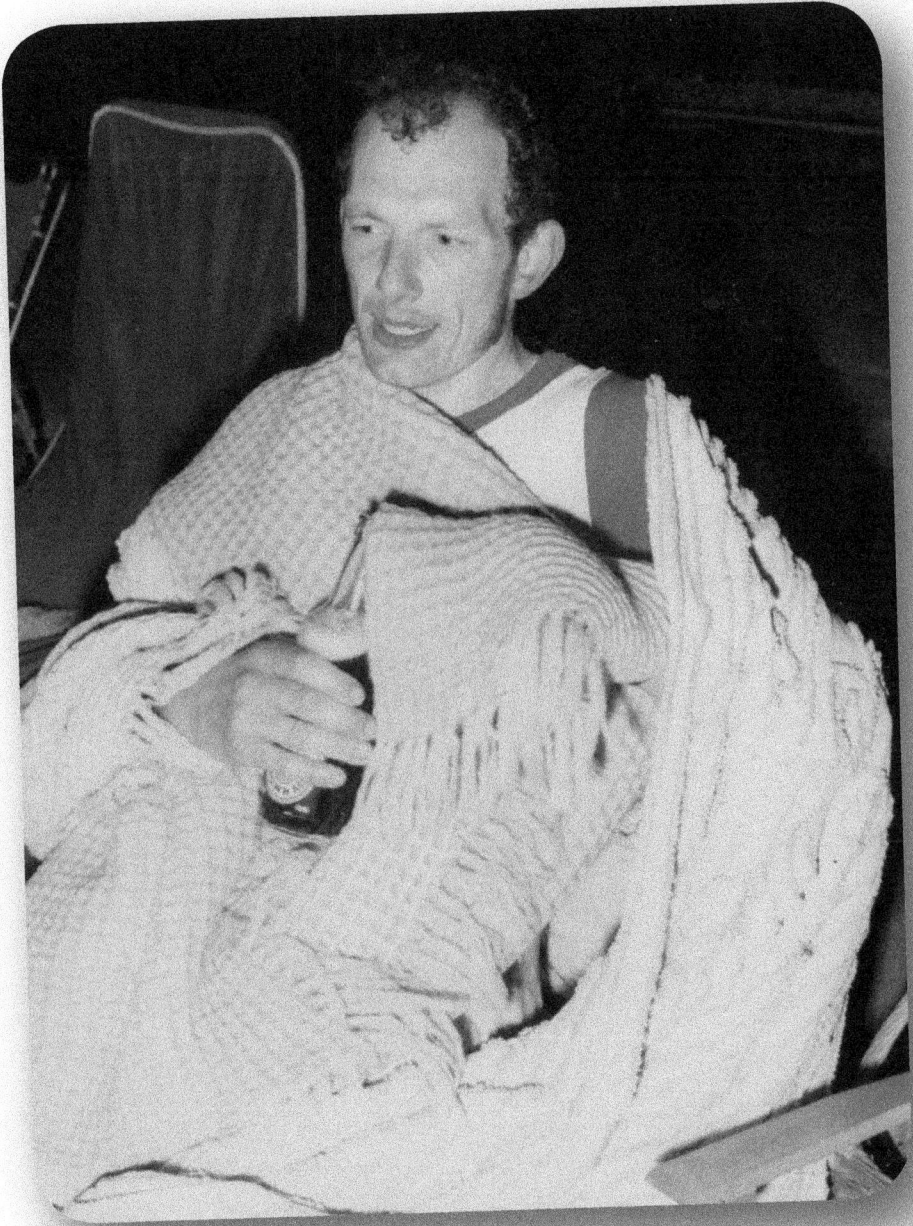

*Just borrowed his wife's best blankets
to watch the rest of the race unfold. "Is
that some beer hidden in there?"*

Roz was still running on, setting the second fastest UK time for 100 miles: 16hrs 33mins 36secs. Both girls were really struggling. Soon after, Lynn looked very tired and had to stop moving! Roz also stopped due to a leg injury. My wife, Bernie (a nurse by profession), had Roz's parents attending to her. Lynn at this point was back on the track again, walking, but Roz wasn't going to give up just yet and started running on the track again, gaining ground every lap on Lynn. Lynn knew Roz was closing the gap and she began to run again. Both of the ladies had now been running for more than 20 hours and the 200km mark slowly appeared for Lynn and yet again another world best for her, going through in 22hrs 15mins 02secs. The previous best was by Sue Medaglia of the USA in a time of 27hrs 49mins 37secs. What a great race this was turning out to be for the girls involved.

Then real drama earlier on… Martin had smashed the 200km world best by 21 minutes in a time of 16hrs 20mins 46secs. As he promptly stepped off the track with 20 minutes to spare, everyone just wanted him to carry on walking a lap or two, but Liz, his wife, couldn't budge him. He had finished with a blazing last lap and that was that. We then realised after the race that he was one lap short.

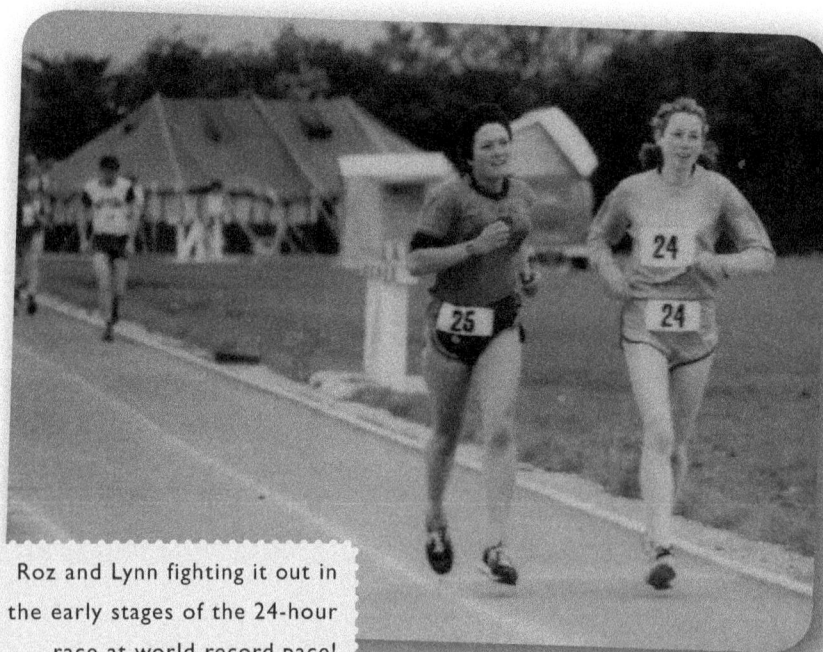

Roz and Lynn fighting it out in the early stages of the 24-hour race at world record pace!

Meanwhile, the men's race was a dual between Mark and Dave. We knew Martin was concentrating on the 200km mark, creating a bigger time gap on Mark in 2nd place. From 130km with a lead of 9 minutes and to 160km now up to 30 minutes ahead. When you think that Mark was ahead of Martin right up to 70km, we were thinking that Mark had perhaps gone off too fast! So could he keep it up? Dave didn't think so in the Gloucester camp.

Ticking along with his effortless stride, Mark in 1st had up to a 25-minute lead on Dave (up to various distances), but at the 170km mark, things began to change! Mark's lead was now from 14-odd minutes at 180km, down to 6mins 10secs. Mark was now in trouble! By the 190-km mark, he has surrendered the lead and by 200km, Dave was ahead by 7mins 08secs, with a total time of 16hrs 58mins 10secs.

The weather was not helping anybody much either. Gusty winds, cold rain it was quite difficult to run in. Little wonder the race looked at times like a battleground, with runners suffering with foot, leg and stomach cramps, and problems physically were adding to the mental problems runners were facing in the latter stages of the race. The tough hill-training schedules the Gloucester squad had gone through in the last six months were paying off!

Dave Dowdle, Chris O'Carroll, Joe Record, with Liz and Martin Daykin cheering them on

Martin was in his tent (snoring his head off), with a world record in the bag and a bottle of beer in his hand. Dave was slowly churning his way into the lead at 200km. Chris at 200k was lying 4th, 20hrs 26mins 55secs, with Ken in 5th, 22hrs 12mins 26secs. Ken was having his own battles keeping the two ladies at bay. Lynn through 200km in 6th with her time of 22hrs 15mins 02secs, only a couple of minutes behind Ken. Roz was 2nd lady through in a time of 22hrs 49mins 02secs in 7th position. Bruce Slade (Exeter) also through in 8th position in a time of 23hrs 09mins 02secs. Nineteen started, and after 200km, eight runners were left contesting for race positions. Four Gloucester AC lads and two ladies, with Mark Pickard and Bruce Slade the remainder.

Edging ever closer to the world record!

(I've switched from mile splits to 10km splits. As runners start to tire, things tend to change quickly in the last few hours.)

At 200km, I made a cardinal error and retired to my tent for a kip. FATAL! Tipton Harriers, who had heard on the media what was happening in Gloucester, had travelled down in convoy to Gloucester to see what was occurring! I remember Ron Bentley of Tipton Harriers telling me, "Worst thing you can do is stop at this point of the race! You'll never get going again." He was right; I could hardly get going. I felt like the tin man from The Wizard of Oz, with no oil. Seemed like ages to get going again! At 210km, five runners were left in it timewise. Dave was increasing his lead all the time, 27mins+ on Mark. Chris was now 3rd, Ken 4th, Lynn through in 5th (1st lady), with 2nd lady Roz still running in 7th position… what a race!

Martin Daykin at his 200km mark 22mins+ inside the existing world record! Who would have thought it would be one lap short on the lap score sheet!

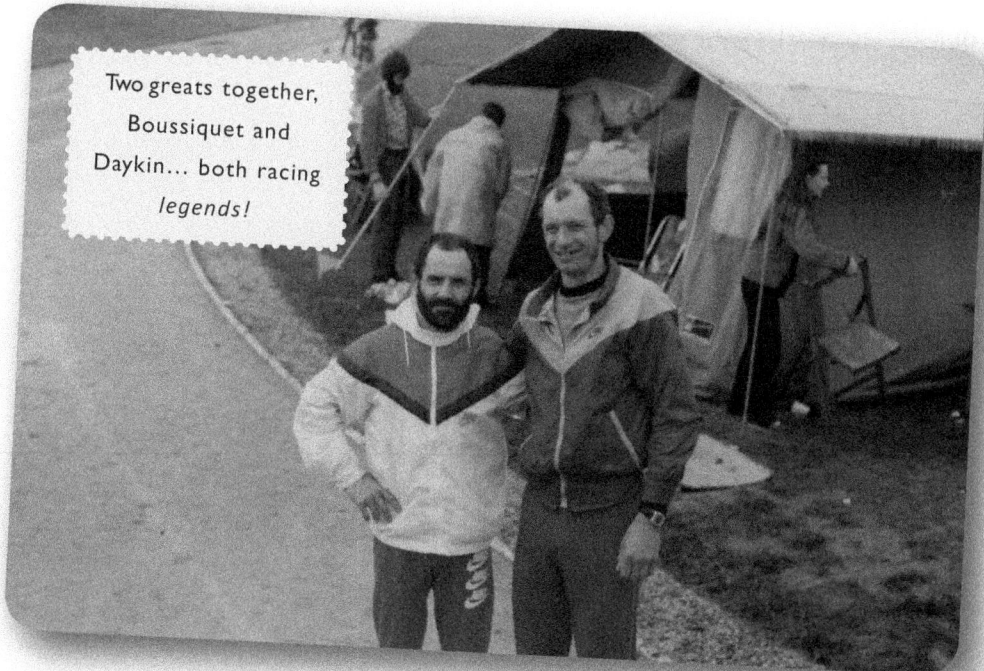

Two greats together, Boussiquet and Daykin... both racing *legends!*

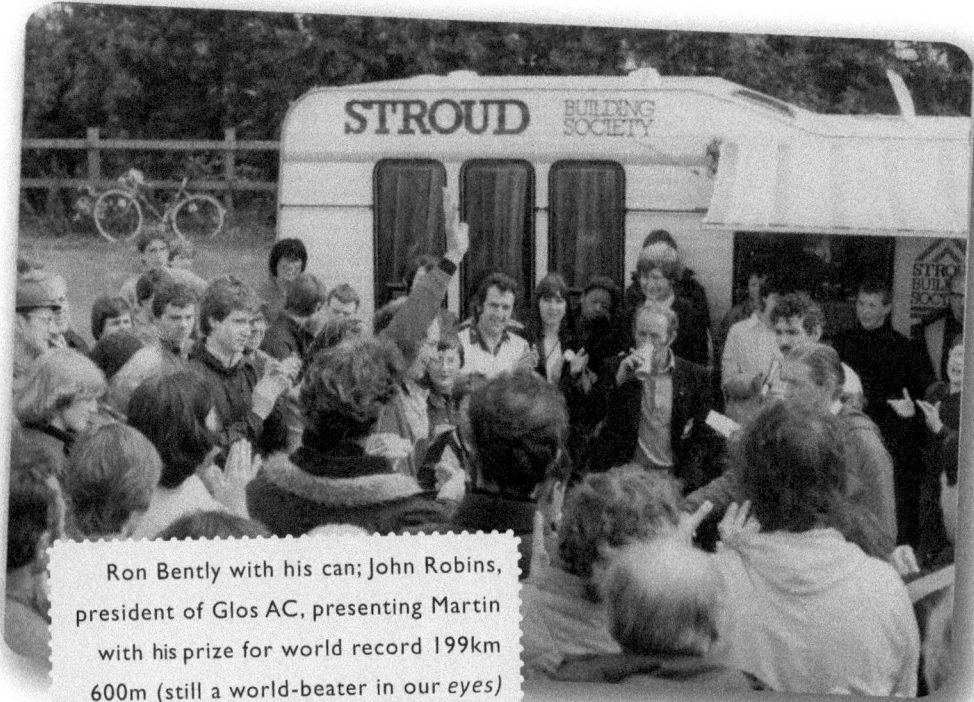

Ron Bently with his can; John Robins, president of Glos AC, presenting Martin with his prize for world record 199km 600m (still a world-beater in our *eyes)*

Martin Daykin collecting his prize!

(Switching back to miles now.)

Dave was still reeling off the miles. 130-mile mark, 25 1/2mins lead, at 140 miles, nearly an hour lead. Mark was really suffering not alternating between running and walking. 150-mile mark, time difference was well over 60mins lead. Mark Pickard's British record looked in danger. Dave had a break and went into his tent. Realising what I was told from Ron Bentley about stopping, I quickly went to Dave's tent and told him not to lie down, just to have a quick change of wet gear, clean socks, etc., to get some fluids and keep moving. I said, "Let's just walk a lap and run a lap and see how it goes."

Dave walked less than a lap and then reeled off another eighteen laps running! He had another stop to drink some fluids and did another twelve laps. Then he remarkably carried on running to the 160-mile mark. His 10-mile split was timed at roughly 96mins; the British record was definitely his for the taking. By now, quite a crowd was building up around the track. Boussiquet and Ron Bently urging Dave on. He staggered through the British record of Mark Pickard's 163-mile 1249yds with over an hour to go! Could he get the world record? Dave was running with incredible consistency, lapping at between 2mins 08secs per 440 laps. From 246km with laps up to 274km, 170 miles+,

Dave Dowdle with his prize 24hr world record!

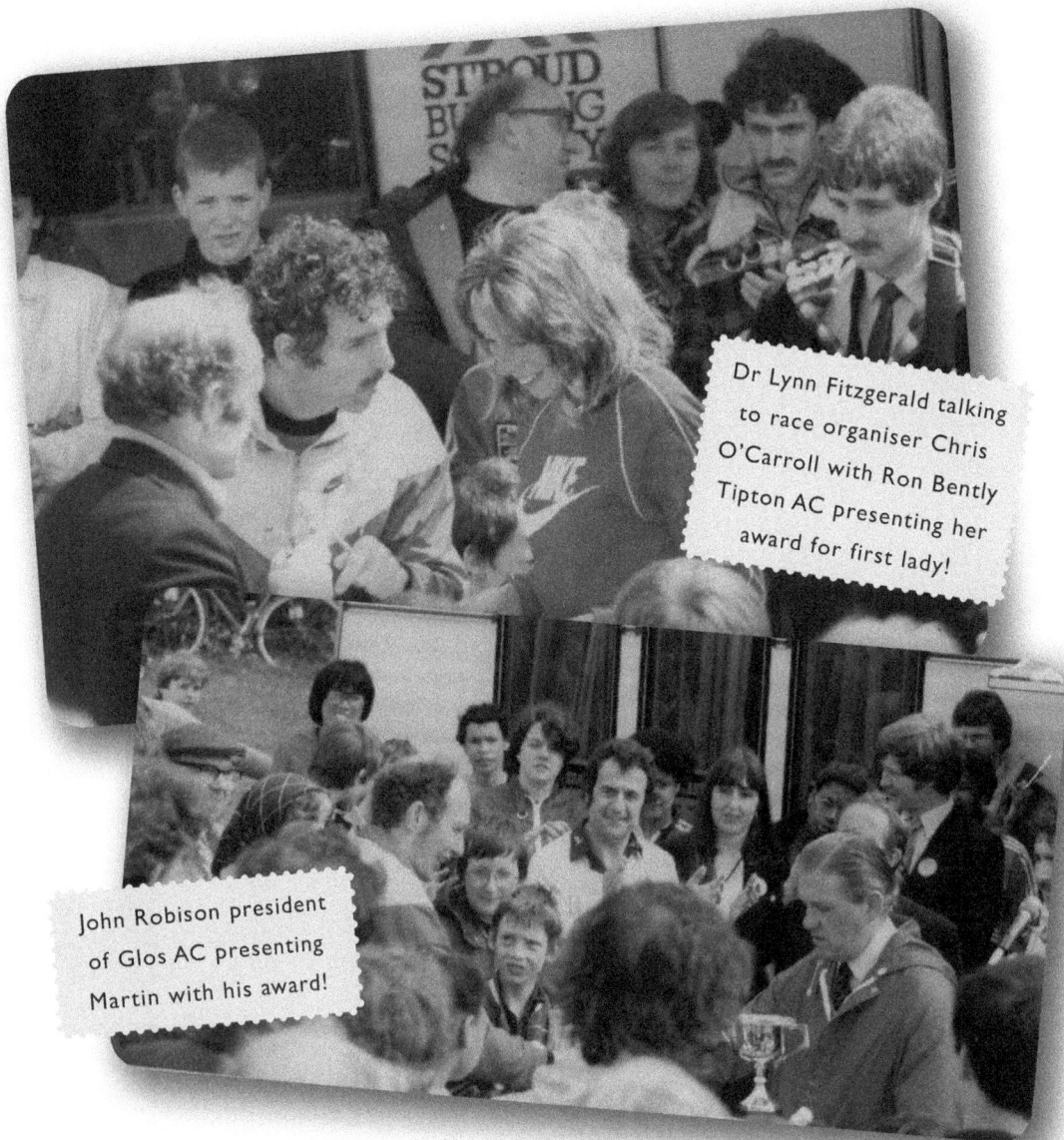

Dr Lynn Fitzgerald talking to race organiser Chris O'Carroll with Ron Bently Tipton AC presenting her award for first lady!

John Robison president of Glos AC presenting Martin with his award!

at hardly any change in time, it was incredible after 23+ hours of running! His early laps were averaging 1min 50secs to 1min 55secs per lap. He never wavered from the start, like a fine-tuned clock in his head. Even up to 70km, he was still approximately on sub 2mins per lap with the odd lap over. From 92km, he started averaging at 2mins to 2mins 10secs per lap, with the odd stop for drinks/change of clothes. Lap after lap, even up to the 24-hour mark, Dave never did more than 2mins 24secs per lap. Incredible consistency and autopilot on from start to finish. He was like a 24-hour Le Mans racing car… but with a bigger engine!

Tipton Harriers and our French friends at the 24hr track race. Ron Bently and Boussiquet, two ultra legends with French ladies. You'd have thought they'd just walked off the catwalk, not been standing in the rain all night by the track!

Boussiquet and Ron Bently having a chat!

Looking at his lap times, he only stopped four times during the whole race!

1. First pit stop at 64 miles+ 8hrs running (total time stopped: 5mins 17secs)
2. Second pit stop at 70 miles+ 9hrs running (total time stopped: 6mins 13secs)
3. Third pit stop at 106 miles+ 14hrs running (total time stopped: 5mins 35secs)
4. Fourth pit stop at 140miles+ 17hrs running (total time stopped: 8mins 26secs)
5. Fifth pit stop: Finish! WORLD RECORD! 171miles+

Dave's total stoppage time: 24mins 59secs in 24 hours, for change of clothes, food and drinks.

Malcolm Cambell Notts AC about to get his award for finishing 10th position, distance of 117m 831yards. Chris O'Carroll trying to figure out how the mic works!

The weather was windy, cold and raining through the night, and a lot of runners succumbed to it and unfortunately failed to finish! It was amazing what all the runners, especially Dave, achieved, considering the circumstances! What a race and what a story!

The Gloucester squad rose to the occasion on the day; two world records, four Gloucester runners in the first eight positions, although Martin went for the 200km world record, so three Glos runners were in the first four.

Both ladies also ran with great distinction! I can see their results could inspire many more ladies having a go at these distances! From 50k+: track, trail and road.

Who would have thought it? We broke English UK, European and world records galore! Our one regret was Jean Gilles Boussiquet having to drop out so early on! The Gloucester squad were hoping to have a real battle with him during our 24hr dual. Although he dropped out early, himself and his supporters stayed throughout the race to cheer on and help out, which was greatly appreciated by all. The Tipton mob came down en masse to cheer and support. The sight of Tipton Harriers' Ron Bently (ex-British 24hr record-holder), with Boussiquet (ex-world 24hr holder) running with Gloucester's Dave Dowdle (soon to be the new world record-holder), was an iconic sight to see!

Hope you enjoyed all the pictures along with the story of the race unfolding. Whether you were spectating, marshalling or timing; thanks to each and every one of you!

"Now who's going to help me put my marquee tent back in the van?"

"See you at the 48-hour track race next year, Chris?"

‖ **"You must be bloody joking!"** ‖

Many a true word spoken in jest... now onto the next race.

Two weeks after our 24-hour race, we were invited to one of France's most prestigious road races. A 100km road race finishing in Paris.

THE STATISTICS   FOR YOU TECK's

TEN MILE 'SPLITS' AND POSITIONS ()

	10M	20M	30M	40M
D.Dowdle	1.15.57 (5)	2.32.08 (3)	3.47.55 (3)	5.04.44 (3)
M.Pickard	1.13.56(=1)	2.27.52 (1)	3.40.42 (1)	4.55.52 (1)
C.O'Carroll	1.25.14(16)	2.45.50(13)	4.03.19(11)	5.20.02 (7)
K.Leyshon	1.21.00(11)	2.37.05(11)	4.01.18(10)	5.31.21(10)
L.Fitzgerald	1.19.12(10)	2.36.33 (9)	3.58.50 (8)	5.21.41 (8)
B.Slade	1.13.56(=1)	2.33.16 (7)	3.54.47 (7)	5.25.45 (9)
R.Paul	1.21.16(13)	2.42.41(12)	4.05.25(12)	5.36.51(11)
M.Daykin	1.16.17 (8)	2.32.07 (2)	3.47.54 (2)	5.04.43 (2)
R.Holmes	1.24.43(15)	2.46.45(15)	4.15.46(14)	5.51.49(12)
M.Campbell	1.22.39(14)	2.56.58(16)	4.30.22(16)	6.15.47(14)
K.Shaw	1.21.05(12)	2.46.31(14)	4.20.05(15)	6.11.46(13)
J.Towers	1.16.35 (9)	2.32.42(=4)	3.53.36 (6)	5.16.04 (6)
B.Clarke	2.08.00(19)	4.21.04(19)	6.39.06(19)	8.52.47(19)
R.Thornton	1.26.08(17)	2.58.34(17)	4.48.50(17)	6.53.05(17)
J.Record	1.16.11 (6)	2.32.47 (6)	3.50.12 (4)	5.10.48 (4)
P.Collins	1.15.48 (4)	2.34.01 (8)	3.59.53 (9)	6.16.11(15)
H.Groon	1.29.54(18)	3.08.32(18)	5.38.33(18)	8.30.35(18)
J.Boussiquet	1.16.15 (7)	2.32.42(=4)	3.50.54 (5)	5.13.27 (5)
D.Choi	1.14.19 (3)	2.36.51(10)	4.14.40(13)	6.17.50(16)

	50M	60M	70M	80M
D.Dowdle	6.22.02 (3)	7.40.55 (3)	9.03.15 (3)	10.28.25 (3)
M.Pickard	6.10.39 (1)	7.27.24 (1)	8.49.18 (1)	10.15.47 (2)
C.O'Carroll	6.38.42 (4)	8.01.31 (4)	9.43.23 (4)	11.09.11 (4)
K.Leyshon	7.05.53(=8)	9.06.39 (9)	10.45.36 (8)	12.24.32 (7)
L.Fitzgerald	6.41.58 (5)	8.18.36 (6)	10.23.44 (6)	12.11.16 (6)
B.Slade	7.05.53(=8)	8.51.10 (7)	10.34.16 (7)	12.50.39 (9)
R.Paul	7.09.42(10)	9.01.28 (8)	10.59.54 (9)	12.41.06 (8)
M.Daykin	6.20.05 (2)	7.38.49 (2)	8.50.19 (2)	10.06.02 (1)
R.Holmes	7.34.22(11)	10.05.13(14)	11.39.46(11)	14.37.29(11)
M.Campbell	8.07.14(14)	10.01.07(13)	12.20.29(12)	14.35.06(10)
K.Shaw	8.39.43(16)	11.09.52(15)	13.31.24(13)	16.09.13(12)
J.Towers	6.44.24 (6)	8.15.40 (5)	9.47.44 (5)	11.19.30 (5)
B.Clarke	11.05.31(18)	13.32.38(18)	16.02.44(16)	18.41.14(15)
R.Thornton	9.06.16(17)	11.43.42(16)	14.35.06(14)	17.27.14(14)
J.Record	7.03.34 (7)	9. 49.08(11)	11.30.09(10)	20.43.56(16)
P.Collins	7.53.33(13)	9.50.54(12)	15.02.13(15)	17.10.58(13)
H.Groon	12.09.04(19)	17.21.20(19)	20.53.11(17)	-
J.Boussiquet	7.35.12(12)	9.47.35(10)	-	-
D.Choi	8.28.08(15)	11.59.12(17)	-	-

	90M	100M	110M	120M
D.Dowdle	11.58.53 (3)	13.28.02 (3)	14.55.52 (3)	16.21.38 (2)
M.Pickard	11.40.30 (2)	13.10.43 (2)	14.49.02 (2)	16.27.46 (3)
C.O'Carroll	12.48.57 (4)	14.19.10 (4)	16.18.41 (4)	19.46.48 (4)
K.Leyshon	14.23.13 (8)	16.01.18 (7)	19.23.51 (6)	21.23.47 (5)
L.Fitzgerald	13.58.48 (6)	15.58.31 (6)	19.07.34 (5)	21.30.31 (6)
B.Slade	15.27.58 (9)	18.03.34 (9)	20.22.57 (8)	22.31.13 (8)
R.Paul	14.20.13 (7)	16.33.36 (8)	20.19.02 (7)	22.01.11 (7)
M.Daykin	11.26.32 (1)	12.48.50 (1)	14.19.17 (1)	15.45.06 (1)
R.Holmes	16.37.04(10)	18.53.26(10)	21.44.33 (9)	-
M.Campbell	17.26.45(11)	19.56.14(11)	22.30.55(10)	-
K.Shaw	18.58.45(12)	21.35.37(12)	23.58.05(11)	-
J.Towers	13.00.45 (5)	14.50.46 (5)	-	-
B.Clarke	20.59.58(14)	23.22.19(13)	-	-
R.Thornton	20.21.40(13)	23.30.53(14)	-	-
J.Record	22.20.32(16)	23.48.52(15)	-	-
P.Collins	21.55.45(15)	-	-	-

TEN MILE 'SPLITS' AND POSITIONS () - continued

	130M	140M	150M	160M
D.Dowdle	17.46.15 (1)	19.09.24 (1)	20.48.30 (1)	22.24.14 (1)
M.Pickard	18.11.49 (2)	20.08.35 (2)	22.19.04 (2)	
C.O'Carroll	21.33.26 (3)	23.43.30 (3)	-	-
K.Leyshon	23.19.02 (4)	-	-	-
L.Fitzgerald	23.22.02 (5)	-	-	-
B.Slade	23.57.45 (6)	-	-	-

	170M
D.Dowdle	23.52.38 (1)

TEN KILOMETRE 'SPLITS' AND POSITIONS ()

	10KM	20KM	30KM	40KM
D.Dowdle	47.15(=5)	1.34.58 (5)	2.21.59 (3)	3.08.54(=2)
M.Pickard	45.56 (3)	1.31.56(=1)	2.17.54 (1)	3.03.18 (1)
C.O'Carroll	52.40(17)	1.46.04(16)	2.35.04(15)	3.23.15(12)
K.Leyshon	50.31(13)	1.39.12(11)	2.26.49(11)	3.17.27(10)
L.Fitzgerald	49.07(11)	1.38.00(10)	2.25.04(10)	3.15.17 (9)
B.Slade	45.34 (1)	1.31.56(=1)	2.22.18(=4)	3.13.12 (8)
R.Paul	51.07(15)	1.40.14(12)	2.31.48(12)	3.22.53(11)
M.Daykin	47.15(=5)	1.34.59(=6)	2.21.58 (2)	3.08.54(=2)
R.Holmes	52.59(16)	1.44.48(13)	2.34.17(14)	3.27.07(14)
M.Campbell	48.32 (9)	1.45.53(15)	2.43.26(16)	3.41.19(16)
K.Shaw	50.08(12)	1.41.04(13)	2.34.01(13)	3.29.48(15)
J.Towers	49.06(10)	1.35.03 (9)	2.22.18(=4)	3.10.51 (6)
B.Clarke	1.19.10(19)	2.38.27(19)	4.01.03(19)	5.26.52(19)
R.Thornton	51.06(14)	1.47.39(17)	2.45.09(17)	3.48.49(17)
J.Record	47.15(=5)	1.34.59(=6)	2.23.04 (8)	3.09.31 (4)
P.Collins	47.15(=5)	1.34.30 (4)	2.22.56 (7)	3.12.28 (7)
H.Groon	53.02(18)	1.51.11(18)	2.56.15(18)	4.25.54(18)
J.Boussiquet	47.14 (4)	1.35.02 (8)	2.22.18(=4)	3.10.32 (5)
D.Choi	45.32 (2)	1.33.08 (3)	2.24.55 (9)	3.24.06(13)

	50KM	60KM	70KM	80KM
Dowdle	3.55.53(=2)	4.43.33(=2)	5.31.31(=2)	6.19.45 (3)
Pickard	3.48.34 (1)	4.35.34 (1)	5.22.12 (1)	6.08.36 (1)
O'Carroll	4.11.49(11)	4.59.07 (8)	5.47.17 (7)	6.36.34 (4)
Leyshon	4.10.18(10)	5.05.44(10)	6.05.10 (9)	7.03.20 (8)
L.Fitzgerald	4.07.21 (8)	4.59.15 (9)	5.51.25 (5)	6.39.51 (5)
B.Slade	4.03.57 (7)	4.59.05 (7)	5.58.18 (8)	7.03.23 (9)
R.Paul	4.14.19(12)	5.08.20(11)	6.06.08(10)	7.06.51(10)
M.Daykin	3.55.53(=2)	4.43.33(=2)	5.31.31(=2)	6.17.47 (2)
R.Holmes	4.24.47(13)	5.27.57(12)	6.25.26(11)	7.31.37(11)
M.Campbell	4.42.08(16)	5.49.04(15)	6.52.32(14)	8.04.04(14)
K.Shaw	4.42.36(15)	5.41.01(13)	7.00.34(15)	8.34.26(16)
J.Towers	4.02.11 (6)	4.51.35 (6)	5.47.23 (4)	6.41.44 (6)
B.Clarke	6.53.25(19)	8.15.05(19)	9.37.07(19)	11.01.43(18)
R.Thornton	4.59.31(17)	6.21.33(17)	7. 43.19(17)	9.03.30(17)
J.Record	3.58.35 (4)	4.48.01 (4)	5.51.43 (6)	7.01.00 (7)
P.Collins	4.10.17 (9)	5.50.50(16)	6.52.17(13)	7.51.10(13)
H.Groon	5.57.58(18)	7.45.29(18)	9.18.44(18)	12.05.18(19)
J.Boussiquet	3.59.24 (5)	4.51.02 (5)	6.43.27(12)	7.32.54(12)
D.Choi	4.26.35(14)	5.44.28(14)	7.07.23(16)	8.24.05(15)

TEN KILOMETRE 'SPLITS' AND POSITIONS () - continued

	90KM	100KM	110KM	120KM
	7.08.50 (3)	7.57.58 (3)	8.50.06 (3)	9.45.26 (3)
Dowdle	6.54.31 (1)	7.43.39 (1)	8.36.55 (1)	9.27.31 (2)
M.Pickard	7.27.58 (4)	8.20.13 (4)	9.29.35 (4)	10.21.10 (4)
C.O'Carroll	8.18.58 (9)	9.25.25 (9)	10.30.37 (8)	11.31.35 (8)
K.Leyshon	7.41.21 (6)	8.39.11 (6)	10.07.40 (6)	11.13.40 (6)
L.Fitzgerald	8.06.06 (7)	9.15.58 (7)	10.19.53 (7)	11.28.57 (7)
B.Slade	8.07.53 (8)	9.23.39 (8)	10.42.11 (9)	11.45.06 (9)
R.Paul	7.06.53 (2)	7.54.38 (2)	8.38.32 (2)	9.23.50 (1)
M.Daykin	9.18.51(13)	10.24.29(13)	11.22.42(11)	12.34.47(10)
R.Holmes	9.22.03(14)	10.24.12(12)	11.53.05(12)	13.09.50(11)
M.Campbell	10.20.07(16)	11.34.02(14)	13.03.21(14)	14.44.14(13)
K.Shaw	7.38.00 (5)	8.35.35 (5)	9.32.49 (5)	10.28.36 (5)
J.Towers	12.30.09(18)	14.07.25(18)	15.33.31(17)	17.10.52(16)
B.Clarke	10.50.18(17)	12.38.09(15)	14.09.01(15)	16.03.55(15)
R.Thornton	8.41.45(10)	10.06.15(11)	11.05.22(10)	13.33.40(12)
J.Record	9.12.00(12)	13.56.10(17)	14.47.10(16)	15.55.27(14)
P.Collins	14.13.48(19)	18.02.23(19)	20.19.20(18)	22.57.38(17)
H.Groon	9.10.58(11)	10.04.10(10)	12.55.34(13)	
J.Boussiquet	10.15.36(15)	12.43.05(16)		
D.Choi				

	130KM	140KM	150KM	160KM
	10.35.03 (3)	11.31.16 (3)	12.27.38 (3)	13.23.07 (3)
D.Dowdle	10.21.51 (2)	11.14.30 (2)	12.07.40 (2)	13.05.52 (2)
M.Pickard	11.16.02 (4)	12.21.54 (4)	13.18.30 (4)	14.14.18 (4)
C.O'Carroll	12.57.47 (9)	13.54.52 (8)	14.58.48 (7)	15.57.12 (7)
K.Leyshon	12.20.45 (6)	13.27.58 (6)	14.34.02 (6)	15.48.36 (6)
L.Fitzgerald	12.57.45 (8)	14.43.36 (9)	16.22.27 (9)	17.58.03 (9)
B.Slade	12.48.25 (7)	13.50.02 (7)	15.24.48 (8)	16.28.00 (8)
R.Paul	10.12.04 (1)	11.02.28 (1)	11.52.19 (1)	12.44.07 (1)
M.Daykin	14.45.59(10)	16.03.07(10)	17.21.40(10)	18.47.36(10)
R.Holmes	14.47.23(11)	16.37.11(11)	18.32.49(11)	19.50.27(11)
M.Campbell	16.21.25(12)	18.00.28(12)	19.59.47(12)	21.30.14(12)
K.Shaw	11.27.06 (5)	12.30.15 (5)	13.35.23 (5)	14.42.10 (5)
J.Towers	18.54.35(15)	20.22.10(14)	21.49.15(14)	23.15.30(13)
B.Clarke	17.39.02(14)	19.36.37(13)	21.35.52(13)	23.21.39(14)
R.Thornton	20.55.10(16)	21.53.24(16)	22.49.16(16)	23.43.40(15)
J.Record	17.24.00(13)	21.14.48(15)	22.47.56(15)	
P.Collins				

	170KM	180KM	190KM	200KM
	14.16.15 (3)	15.11.26 (3)	16.05.03 (2)	16.58.10 (2)
D.Dowdle	14.01.39 (2)	15.05.16 (2)	16.09.21 (3)	17.05.18 (3)
M.Pickard	15.35.42 (4)	16.40.51 (4)	17.55.59 (4)	20.26.55 (4)
C.O'Carroll	18.29.25 (8)	19.45.16 (6)	21.06.13 (5)	22.12.26 (5)
K.Leyshon	18.03.23 (7)	19.35.54 (5)	21.09.18 (6)	22.15.02 (6)
L.Fitzgerald	19.19.59 (9)	20.40.15 (7)	22.07.56 (8)	23.09.02 (8)
B.Slade	17.42.35 (6)	20.41.54 (8)	21.41.56 (7)	22.49.34 (7)
R.Paul	13.37.05 (1)	14.35.03 (1)	15.28.24 (1)	16.20.46 (1)
M.Daykin	20.39.48(10)	22.16.37 (9)	23.46.44 (9)	-
R.Holmes	21.09.33(11)	22.57.37(10)	-	
M.Campbell	23.06.20(12)	-		
K.Shaw	15.59.03 (5)	-		
J.Towers				

	210KM	220KM	230KM	240KM
	17.51.24 (1)	18.42.26 (1)	19.41.10 (1)	20.40.15 (1)
D.Dowdle	18.18.29 (2)	19.28.24 (2)	20.47.10 (2)	22.06.29 (2)
M.Pickard	21.41.22 (3)	23.06.18 (3)	-	-
C.O'Carroll	23.25.58 (4)	-		
K.Leyshon	23.27.25 (5)			
L.Fitzgerald				

	250KM	260KM	270KM
	21.42.10 (1)	22.38.23 (1)	23.32.34 (1)
D.Dowdle	23.36.10 (2)		
M.Pickard			

FOR YOU STATISIONS APPRUIA

GLOUCESTER AC 24 HOURS TRACK RUNNING RACE at Blackbridge, Podsmead, Gloucester
on 22/23 May 1982 (starting at 10 am)

RESULT:

1.	DAVE DOWDLE	Gloucester AC	274.880 kms	170m 1412y WR
2.	MARK PICKARD	Epsom and Ewell Harriers	253.138 kms	157m 515y
3.	CHRIS O'CARROLL	Gloucester AC	228.065 kms	141m 1254y
4.	KEN LEYSHON	Gloucester AC	215.271 kms	133m 1343y
5.	LYNN FITZGERALD (Lady)	Highgate Harriers	214.902 kms	133m 939y WR
6.	BRUCE SLADE	Exeter Harriers	209.659 kms	130m 485y
7.	ROS PAUL (Lady)		208.201 kms	129m 651y
8.	MARTIN DAYKIN	Gloucester AC	200.000 kms	124m 482y WR
9.	BOB HOLMES	Notts AC	192.770 kms	119m 1375y
10.	MALCOLM CAMPBELL	Notts AC	189.054 kms	117m 831y
11.	KEN SHAW	Cambridge Harriers	177.520 kms	110m 538y
12.	JOHN TOWERS	East Hull Harriers	173.200 kms	107m 1093y
13.	BROMLEY CLARKE	Berryhill AC	165.683 kms	102m 1673y
14.	RICHARD THORNTON	Salisbury AC	164.243 kms	102m 98y
15.	JOE RECORD	AUSTRALIA	162.880 kms	101m 367y
16.	PAUL COLLINS	Highgate Harriers	160.284 kms	99m 1048y
17.	HERB GROON	USA	128.412 kms	79m 1393y
18.	JEAN GILLES BOUSSIQUET	St. Pierre D'Amilly, FRANCE	112.000 kms	69m 1044y
19.	DON CHOI	California, USA	105.600 kms	65m 1085y

The following performances are being put forward for ratification as records:

World Best Performance, UK (all comers) Best Performance and UK (National)
Best Performance:

24 Hours running:	Dave Dowdle	274.880 kms	(170m 1412y)
24 Hours running (Women):	Lynn Fitzgerald	214.902 kms	(133m 939y)
50 miles (Women):	Lynn Fitzgerald	6 hours 41 mins 58 secs	
100 kilometres (Women):	Lynn Fitzgerald	8 hours 39 mins 10 secs	
150 kilometres (Women):	Lynn Fitzgerald	14 hours 34 mins 2 secs	
200 kilometres (Women):	Lynn Fitzgerald	22 hours 15 mins 0 secs	
200 kilometres:	Martin Daykin	16 hours 20 mins 46 secs	WR

UK (All comers) Best Performance and UK (National) Best Performance:

100 miles (Women):	Lynn Fitzgerald	15 hours 48 mins 15 secs.

The Race Secretary: Chris O'Carroll, 11 Grasmere Road, Longlevens, Gloucester
(Gloucester 22382)
Extra copies of this result sheet can be obtained by sending a stamped addressed
envelope to Don Turner, 40 Rosedale Road, Stoneleigh, Epsom, Surrey KT17 2 JH

R A C E 8

After all the excitement and first experience of our 24hr track race in May, the Gloucester squad were invited to run in one of France's supposedly most prestigious races, namely a 100km race to Paris with the grand title of:

Les 100km De La Division Leclerc
5/6 June 1982
(Just over two weeks after the 24hr race)

This sounded like a very grand occasion! We gracefully accepted their invitations and set off to Paris; still on a high from our 24-hour race previously. We travelled over to Paris in two cars. First car was Martin and his brother Tony, Liz (Martin's wife) and fellow athlete Dennis Weir. In the second car was young Gloucester AC member Phil Hoddy (1min 50sec 800m runner), who was our driver, along with Dave, Ken and myself travelling.

Talk about a major bust-up! The whole scenario was chaos from start to finish, both before, during and after (finishing with a big bang!).

Martin wrote a story about his experience doing the whole race, starting from Rambouillet, to Paris. The whole race turned into a comedy show. We can laugh about it now, but it wasn't so funny at the time.

Hope you find it funny reading Martin's account. There are more stories to follow after Martin's tale, with the rest of the Gloucester squad's experiences later on in Paris!

RECORD FOUR IN PARIS

GLOUCESTER'S RECORD-BREAKING FOURSOME, Dave Dowdle, Martin Daykin, Chris O'Carroll and Ken Leyshon will sample world acclaim this weekend when they run in France's premier 100km race, the Division Leclerc in Paris.

Pint-sized Dave Dowdle is guaranteed star billing. His staggering run in Gloucester's recent 24-hour race, which set a new world best of 170 miles, has captivated the French.

On the continent ultra-distance runners are greatly admired, and the French are clamouring to see the man who destroy their own legend of road and track, Jean Gilles Boussiquet. Boussiquet held the world record until Dowdle's assault, two years ago.

The 100km distance (62 miles) is also not favourable to Dowdle's usual work load. With a weekly training programme of almost 250 miles, the shorter distance may well be too fast for Dowdle, who thrives on the more demanding 24-hour, and 100 mile treks.

The distance could well favour Gloucester's other world record holder, Martin Daykin. The 35-year-old is the current 200km record holder, and has also triumphed at the 100km barrier. He was the world's fastest in 1980, and last year recorded the second best time for 1981.

Daykin certainly realises that the world record is vulnerable.

"There is at least another hour to come off the current world best. That was shown in 1980 when I took 20 minutes off the previous best. In any other sport such a reduction would be laughable, and physically impossible."

DAYKIN ON THE CONTINENT

Martin Daykin

The French ultra-distance dream took a bit of a knock on 6th June in the division Leclerc 100 kilometres between Rambouillet and Paris. Our party of twelve had been promised free accommodation and reimbursement for ferry and petrol costs, but it was only after hours of haggling and threats that we would not run, that English organiser Jack Pinney was made to keep to his word.

Even so, we eventually found ourselves 'sleeping' on the floors of two hotel rooms. Sleep was impossible due to a noisy wedding party directly opposite our rooms.

Our attitude as we lined up for the 4 am start with no sleep or breakfast was less than enthusiastic.

Early leaders were Colmar and Gaudin, the former running true to form by reaching 10km 2 minutes ahead of the field and hitting the wall at 20km. I settled for tracking Gaudin, just two metres behind him. I gave myself absolutely no chance of finishing as a result of all the pre-race trauma, and decided on hanging on for as long as possible.

Gaudin steadfastly ignored me for a while and set a cracking pace. By 25km, we were several minutes ahead of anyone

else, and the only company we had was the course car and Gaudin's cyclist, plus the occasional appearance of my brother Tony with my drinks.

Soon after this, Gaudin did a silly thing. He deliberately ran in the centre of the narrow road to prevent my brother coming past in his car. When Tony eventually did get past, Gaudin seemed incensed that I had a helper in the car. Tony was followed by a convoy of Gaudin's other helpers in their cars! When he summoned a police motorcyclist and demanded that I be disqualified, I lost my temper.

The 2-metre gap closed to inches and I read his horoscope for him, with a liberal sprinkling of colloquial French. For a while, there was the strange scene of a Frenchman being pursued by an Englishman, weaving from side to side of the road as the former tried to escape the flow of invective, followed by a cyclist fearful for his charge's safety, while all the while, the course car some 50 metres ahead played 'Misty' over its loudspeaker, blissfully ignorant of the events behind.

The marathon was reached on 2:34 shortly followed by 50km in just under 3:07. For the first time, I moved alongside

Gaudin. He still wanted to lead so I made sure I was just a fraction ahead of him, just to unsettle him. This was a great duel, but at 70 kilometres, he spoiled it by starting to apologise for his early behaviour, plus some other little tricks he had been pulling, and asked if I could help him to break the French record!

My answer was to increase the pace and encourage him to follow, saying that it was 'easy' if he kept with me. There was soon a gap of 2 minutes, which seemed to delight the French enthusiasts following the race. It was at this moment that Tony got himself lost on the course, and just when I needed drinks the most, I had to go without.

He caught me up just after the 75km feed station, with the tales of all our party plus our drivers, plus most of the rest of the field going off course. After 70 kilometres, there were just no arrows or marshals. Mark Pickard lost about 20 minutes; Dave Dowdle was seen going the wrong way down a motorway. Chris O'Carroll also lost time, as did my wife, Liz, and Phil Hoddy in the other two cars.

John Towers was getting dangerously low on fluids, but thankfully Liz found him with nothing more serious than a swollen tongue. Dennis (Walkies) Weir was the only one of our party who insisted he had not got lost, but after tales of bands he had seen en route, which the few of us who had gone the right way hadn't seen, we were doubtful.

Up front, I had recovered from slight dehydration and had the course car alongside me to protect me from the whirlwind Paris traffic. Tony was able to move up occasionally to pass feed bottles and big plastic bottles full of water to pour over my head. The 80-km point was reached in exactly 5 hours and I still felt surprisingly good. By 85km, however, I could feel the start of fatigue and I was pushing it on for the first time. Shortly after this, a Renault Five decided to overtake the course car on the inside. Too late, he saw that I was in the space and locked his wheels up at high speed. A leap that Lynn Davies would have been proud of was followed by a display of feed bottle- throwing that any serious football supporter would have been proud of.

Right on target, the bottle hit the boot with the force of an Exocet missile. The driver saw my approaching form and left at high speed through a red light. The course car occupants could understand my well-chosen phrases, and windows were wound up to protect tender ears, and once again, 'Misty' was played at high volume.

John Towers was hit by a driver turning right, who amused himself by clouting John with his hand, somewhere below the belt. When John had picked himself up, he injured his hand… by putting dents in the car's boot and bonnet. The frightened occupant drove off through a red light with a French policeman assuring John that he had seen everything and had the car's number.

Nearer the centre, the traffic became more chaotic, but luckily, the police motorcycle escort was going on ahead and stopping any traffic from crossing my path. Tony did a magnificent job of driving with his elbows as he continually filled feed bottles on the move. I calculated a finish time of about 6:25 and was by 95km getting giddy turns. French enthusiasts joined Tony in passing me water bottles to pour on my head and said my lead was now about 6 minutes.

Still playing 'Misty', the course car guided me to the statue of General Leclerc, where the race abruptly finished. Not seeing any of the usual end-of-race banners, I was unsure where the line was and I had an army of pressmen and race officials chasing after me in an attempt to convince me that I really had finished.

The time was given as 6:15:42. The time coincided with my watch, but it didn't feel like 100km. Gaudin eventually crossed the line in 6:22:17, also expressing disbelief as to the distance. We both agreed it was about 3km short.

There were splendid cups and trophies and the Gloucester Ultra-Distance 'Hit Squad' got the team prize. It was more a prize for navigation than for running! There were even runners coming to the finish in the wrong direction.

Mark finished in 5th place, closely followed by Chris in 10th, John Towers 11th, Dave Dowdle 12th and Dennis 13th. With no accommodation arranged for us, we returned to Dover, stopping only to reduce the contents of French marathon runner Yves Seigneuric's beer cellar. As we continued on our way, the radio was turned off, just in case that damned tune 'Misty' came on again!

Martin Daykin, winner
100km Division, Leclerc

⊃ RESULTS

1.	M. Daykin	6hrs 15mins 42secs
2.	B. Gaudin	6hrs 23mins 17secs
3.	A. Guignard	6hrs 57mins 0secs
4.	R. Lesaure	
5.	M. Pickard	
6.	G. Courmont	
7.	P. Gonzales	
8.	P. Barbieri	
9.	F. Tonneau	
10.	C. O'Carroll	7hrs 42mins 08secs
11.	J. Towers	
12.	D. Dowdle	8hrs 08mins 26secs
13.	D. Weir	

Approximately 350 started.

Martin Daykin's account of this race, in which he details exactly what happened, is most instructive, especially to those who venture abroad. While the majority of these events are satisfactory and our many athletes who compete in continental races find these well worthwhile and enjoyable, there is always the chance of hitting a bad one.

Perhaps we have the right to feel a little proud that breaches of good sportsmanship do not occur amongst the members of the road-running fraternity in the UK.

RECORD FOUR IN PARIS

GLOUCESTER'S RECORD-BREAKING FOURSOME, Dave Dowdle, Martin Daykin, Chris O'Carroll and Ken Leyshon will sample world acclaim this weekend when they run in France's premier 100km race, the Division Leclerc in Paris.

Pint-sized Dave Dowdle is guaranteed star billing. His staggering run in Gloucester's recent 24-hour race, which set a new world best of 170 miles, has captivated the French.

On the continent ultra-distance runners are greatly admired, and the French are clamouring to see the man who destroyed their own legend of road and track, Jean Gilles Boussiquet. Boussiquet held the world record until Dowdle's assault, two years ago.

It is as yet uncertain whether or not Dowdle will race. He caught a chill last week, and he is still not 100 per cent fit. He may well use the event as a promotional appearance, his presence alone being sufficient for the fanatical French.

The 100km distance (62 miles) is also not favourable to Dowdle's usual work load. With a weekly training programme of almost 250 miles, the shorter distance may well be too fast for Dowdle, who thrives on the more demanding 24-hour, and 100 mile treks.

The distance could well favour Gloucester's other world record holder, Martin Daykin. The 35-year-old is the current 200 record holder, and has also triumphed at the 100km barrier. He was the world's fastest in 1980, and last year recorded the second best time for 1981.

Vulnerable

Daykin certainly realises that the world record is vulnerable.

"There is at least another hour to come off the current world best. That was shown in 1980 when I took 20 minutes off the previous best. In any other sport such a reduction would be laughable, and physically impossible."

WORLD BEST FOR MARTIN DAYKIN?

Gloucester AC ultra-distance star Martin Daykin won the Division Leclerc 100km road race from Rambouillet to Paris on June 6th in 6:15.42 which, if the course is accurate, represents a world best for a road race at this distance. Martin writes: "I should have run that race in about 6:35 with the warmish conditions later in the race and the slightly undulating nature of the course. However I was in a BAD mood (because of various problems with the organisation etc) and that time was achieved on sheer venom and a determination to succeed in spite of everything".

1, M. Daykin (Glouc) 6:15.42; 2, B. Gaudin 6:23:17; 3, A. Guignard 6:57:00; 4, R. Lesayre 7:01:58; 5, M. Pickard (E&E) 7:02.52 . . . 10, C. O'Carroll (Glouc) 7:42:08; 11, J. Towers (E. Hull) 7:45:20; 16, D. Dowdle (Glouc) 8:08.26; 17, D. Weir (Sale) 8:09.37.

ATHLETICS WEEKLY : 14.8.82.

DAYKIN'S WORLD RECORD

IN a race filled with drama, Martin Daykin, one of Gloucester's ultra distance running stars, set a new world record in winning a 100 kilometres (62 mile) race in Paris.

Daykin was first home in a field of 350 and set a new world best of six hours, 15 minutes and 40 seconds. After battling it out with French champion Gaudin, Daykin pulled away in the late stages and won in the gruelling, hot conditions by more than eight minutes.

Gloucester won the team prize, but there were some

CITIZEN 9.6.82.

anxious moments for the squad, when Dave Dowdle, the world's best over 24 hours, went off the course.

Second City man home was Chris O'Carroll, who is slowly moving up into world class, finishing in eighth place and knocking 23 minutes off his personal best in a time of seven hours, 36 minutes, 20 seconds. This was despite going off the course at one point due to bad race directions.

Rescue mission

The Gloucester team anxiously awaited their third man home, but word got around that Dowdle had got hopelessly lost and was spotted running off down the main Paris motorway.

Ken Leyshon, the fourth Gloucester runner who had earlier pulled out with stomach

trouble, went into action on a rescue mission. He got a lift to Dowdle and directed him back onto the right route.

Both of them were suffering due to a lack of drinks, but team manager, Phil Hoddy, Tony Daykin and Martin's wife, Liz, got out to Dowdle and Leyshon with drinks and sponges just in time.

Despite suffering, Dowdle managed to hobble in to finish in 16th in eight hours, one minute, 40 seconds. This gave Gloucester the team prize with record 25 points and it was a proud day for the team as they received their trophies from the French Minister of Sport.

Their efforts were all the more remarkable as they were still recovering from their exertions in the City's 24 hour race two weeks ago.

-=-   CLASSEMENT DE LA COURS DES 100 KMS de LA   -=-
DIVISION LECLERC

JUST THE GLOS FINISHER TO PRUT
+ 1st TEAM

1. DAYKIN Martin *UK*	6h.15' 42" ✗	35. BERGNER Françis	8h.56'49"
2. GAUDIN Bernard	6h.23' 17"	36. MASSONIERE J.Paul	9h.03'28"
3. GUIGNARD André	6h.57'	37. LE CALVEZ Yves	9h.08'15"
4. LeSAVRE René	7h.01' 58"	38. BOUFFLET Patrick	9h.15'05"
5. PICKARD Mark *UK*	7h.02' 52"	39. RIGOIR Olivier	9h.15'15"
6. COURMONT Gérard	7h.05' 52"	40. PASTUREAU Claude	9h.18'10"
7. GONZALEZ Pierre	7h.25' 32"	41. BOURREZ Alain	9h.25'50"
8. BARBIERI Pierre	7h.26' 32"	42. LE CALVEZ Loïc	9h.27'38"
9. TONNEAU Fernand *UK*	7h.36' 34"	43. LECUYER Alain	9h.29'5"
10. O'CARROLL Christopher	7h.42' 08" ✗	44. LE HOIZAN Maurice	9h.38'15"
11. TOWERS John *UK*	7h.45' 20"	45. LE RICHE J.F.	9h.42'56"
12. CREISSELS Denis	7h.50' 20"	46. LHUILLIER Daniel	9h.43'30"
13. DUBEUF François	7h.50' 35"	47. LHOMER Monique	9h.47'00"
14. GROSBOIS Guy	7h.51' 53"	48. RATHERY Serge	9h.49'45"
15. HUET Patrick	8h.00' 17"	49. COUCHE Edith	9h.51' 55"
16. DOWDLE DAVID *UK*	8h.08' 26" ✗	50. COLMAR Guy	9h.53' 25"
17. WEIR Denis *UK*	8h.09' 37"	51. ZELTZER Lucien	9h.57' 22"
18. MEUNIER Jean-Pierre	8h.17' 30"	52. BRICHE Guy	9h.55' 03"
19. TISSOT Patirck	8h.20' 41"	53. BOULET J.Claude	10h.01' 37"
20. MISERY Pierre	8h.25' 42"	54. FABRE Eric	10h.04' 33
21. BOISSONEAU J.François	8h.26'07"	55. LAHMAR	10h.04' 33"
22. EVENO Gérard	8h.27' 40"	56. CASPARIUS Philippe	10h.07' 14"
23. CRIBIER Jacques	8h.27' 40"	57. LANQUILLE Michel	10h.12' 48"
24. SCHORI Alain	8h.29' 00"	58. PHILIPPOT Joseph	10h.15' 45"
25. LAFEYE José	8h.39'04"	59. LONG Guy	10h.16' 25"
26. MANDON Gilbert	8h.39'25"	60. CZAJA J.Claude	10h.17' 52"
27. DENIAU François	8h.40'08"	61. GERMAIN Alexandre	10h.23' 20"
28. BERTHON René Jean	8h.44'53"	62. PICOT Pierre	10h.25' 32"
29. CURTY Jean	8h.45'08"	63. ISSANCHOU Christian	10h.26'37"
30. JACQUET Jacques	8h.49'10"	64. HUMBERT Serge	10h.34' 13"
31. LEROY Bernard	8h.49'20"	65. RUSSIAS Pierre	10h.36' 22"
32. SPINGER Gérard	8h.51'03"	66. DECLERCK Jean	10h.38' 26"
33. VERVILLE Christian	8h.56'20"	67. RACHMART J.Marc	10h.38' 26"
34. POIRAY René	8h.56'28"	68. ARRAULT J.Pierre	10h.41' 25"

LEYSNOUKEN DNF.   1st TEAM 27 PTS, TEAM OF 3
TO FINISH.

Martin's story more or less conveyed what a sorry state the whole race was! I remember coming into the Paris suburbs totally lost, then I had to ask a French lady, "Is this the way to the Paris city centre?" The lady directed me towards the right direction! Shortly after, I spotted a runner and took off after him. I was so relieved to see another runner and said immediately to him, "Where are we, mate? How far is it to go?" He was a French runner who shrugged his shoulders, saying something in French! It slowly dawned on me that he was also lost. What a bloody mess! Eventually, I met up with another Frenchman who lived in Paris… thank God I was saved, and finally I tottered in to finish!

Ken was already in along with Martin, or so I thought! Ken heard that a little funny Englishman was seen running down the main Parisian motorway, towards Paris! Ken, who was also lost at the time, frantically flagged a police car down and explained what was happening! So together with sirens blazing, they tore down the Paris streets to pick him up! Poor Dave thought he was being arrested, but they escorted him back to where he went the wrong way and pointed out the right way (he still got lost again later on), but he finally made it to the finish in one piece.

Ken by then had had enough, dropped out and got a lift to the finish, but due to Ken's unselfish act, we still won the overall team prize. Three to score, so including Martin's victory as well, it turned out not too bad after all!

Martin and Liz then decided to drive back to Calais straight away, while Phil, Ken, Dave and myself decided to do some sightseeing in Paris and visit the Eiffel Tower, which none of us had visited before!

Having recovered from our exploits and been up to the top of the Eiffel Tower and back down again, we were walking back to the car when there was a loud explosion across the river opposite the tower. We could hear police cars and ambulances coming towards us at a rapid rate. They rushed by us to go over the next bridge right and then turn left, to roar by us up the road opposite us across the river! This was also the same road we would be taking to get us back onto the road to the Calais ferry. We knew that before long Paris would be gridlocked.

I said to Phil (our driver), "When the police and ambulances come by, nip in behind them over the bridge. When you see directions to Calais, nip left; otherwise, we will be here all day long!"

Down roared more emergency vehicles, so Phil took his opportunity to nip smartly behind them over the bridge. The French traffic, which had parted left and right, had rumbled what we were doing and started honking their horns and shaking their fists at us.

"Where's the sign, Phil?"

"Not yet, Chris."

"Oh God, there it is, quick yank left, signs for Calais, thank goodness… now drive on out of here and stop at the first quiet spot."

I think we had had enough excitement for one day, what with the race fiasco and now some kind of bomb going off. We definitely needed a cup of tea by this point.

We later learned that it had, in fact, been a bank that was blown up further on up the road from our left turn to Calais.

Let's go home, boys!

Our next race was the old favourite: Two Bridges Race, Rosyth, Scotland. This was to be our fourth visit, but also our last!

R A C E 9

Two Bridges Race, Rosyth
28 August 1982

Our ninth ultra race together. Gloucester AC had accumulated several new members, with a record seven members running for us!

This particular race also had a record entry and it was a lovely sunny day… what more could you ask for!

The Fifteenth Two Bridges Road Race
28 August 1982

A record field of 115 starters for this 36-mile race in Scotland were sent on their way by Provost Les Wood at 10 am on Saturday 28th August. Immediately, Charlie Trayer, the strong challenger from Reading (USA) set off alone in front of a group of five, comprising Martin Daykin (Gloucester AC), Tim Johnstone (Portsmouth AC), John Watkins (South London Harriers) and the Fife A.B pair Sam Graves and Bob Pemble. The group reached the 5-mile mark in 28mins, 25secs, with Trayer 13 seconds ahead. In the run through Culross to Longanett, against a strong west wind, the chasing group dropped Pemble but were joined by Clive Rutland (Banbury Harriers).

Chris O'Carroll (Gloucester AC) joined the leading group approaching 10 miles (56mins 59secs). After crossing the Kincardine Bridge, the group reached 15 miles in 1hr 26mins, 07secs, over flat terrain and with a following wind.

The pace now increased and Johnston and Daykin forged ahead, with the first reaching 20 miles in 1hr 53mins, 18secs, just a minute ahead of Daykin. Watkins, Rutland, Graves and Trayer were up to 3 minutes behind the leader.

The gap between Johnston and Daykin widened up the first and only steep hill on the course. Tim Johnston, who was 8th in the 1968 Olympic Marathon in Mexico City and now at 41 a veteran, led Daykin by 2 1/2 minutes at 25 miles (2-28-17).

Having recently failed to finish the Woodford to Southend race, he was determined to do better, and he kept to a sensible pace to maintain the same lead at 30 miles (2-50-54). Behind, Dave Francis (Fife AC) and Les Davis (Gloucester AC) were both making a strong move forward, while the American Charlie Trayer, after a few difficult miles, recovered and was moving nearer to John Watkins, still holding 3rd place at 30 miles.

Crossing the Forth Road Bridge, it looked doubtful as to whether the leader could hold on to become the first veteran to win the race, as Daykin was gaining on him at every mile and finishing strongly. However, hang on he did, to reach the finish at the Rosyth Service Sports Centre in 3hrs 28mins 36secs, just 32 seconds ahead of Daykin, who had taken all places from 2nd to 5th in four successive years. Watkins held on to 3rd place, 3 minutes ahead of Charlie Trayer, who became the highest placed overseas competitor in the history of this event.

The team trophy was won for the first time by Gloucester AC (31 points), with Fife AC second and Tipton Harriers third.

A record 104 runners completed the course.

1	T. Johnson (V)	Portsmouth AC	3hrs 28mins 36secs
2	M. Daykin	Gloucester AC	3hrs 29mins 08secs
3	J. Watkins	South London Harriers	3hrs 35mins 16secs
4	C. A. Trayer	Reading RRC (USA)	3hrs 38mins 18secs
5	D. Francis	Fife AC	3hrs 43mins 06secs
6	L. Davis	Gloucester AC	3hrs 43mins 20secs
7	C. Rutland	Banbury Harriers	3hrs 44mins 13secs
8	M. Reid	Victoria Park Harriers	3hrs 46mins 08secs
9	R. S. Dalby	Harrowgate AC	3hrs 47mins 44secs
10	G. Kay (V)	Stafford AC	3hrs 48mins 25secs
11	P. D. Taylor	Woodstock Harriers	3hrs 50mins 02secs
12	S. L. C. Graves	Fife AC	3hrs 51mins 48secs
13	M. Williams	Tidewater Striders (USA)	3hrs 52mins 02secs
14	A. Hardy	Burnham Joggers AC	3hrs 52mins 34secs
15	W. G. Humphries	South London Harriers	3hrs 53mins 36secs
16	K. Leyshon	Gloucester AC	3hrs 55mins 26secs
17	W. Carr	Tipton Harriers	3hrs 55mins 43secs
18	D. West (V)	Victoria Park Harriers	3hrs 56mins 02secs
19	J. Galvin	Leigh Park Harriers	3hrs 57mins 20secs
20	J. E. Cock (V)	Epsom and Ewell AC	3hrs 57mins 23secs
21	A. Stirling	Bo'ness Harriers	3hrs 57mins 38secs
22	J. Cotterill	Tipton Harriers	3hrs 58mins 26secs
23	D. Dowdle	Gloucester AC	3hrs 59mins 22secs

Another great result for the Glos Team! First time in four years we finally won the team award.

AWARDS

1st	Gloucester AC – A Team	
2nd	Fife AC – A Team	
3rd	Tipton Harriers – A Team	
1st	Gloucester AC – B Team	
2nd	Bolton – B Team	
3rd	Tipton Harriers – B Team	

A double celebration for Gloucester AC. Individual positions as follows:

- A. 2nd Martin Daykin 3hrs 29mins 08secs (Outstanding run again)
- A. 6th L.Davis 3hrs 43mins 20secs (New member, great first run)
- A. 16th K. Leyshon 3hrs 55mins 26secs (A personal PB by minutes)
- B. 23rd D. Dowdle 3hrs 59mins 22secs (Not at his best, but still a strong run)
- B. 31st J. Conlon 4hrs 10mins 01secs (First time ultra, fine run)
- B. 76th T.Whitefoot 4hrs 57mins 13secs (New to this race, also a fine run)

Chris O'Carroll unfortunately dropped out at 25 miles at a time of 2hrs 29mins 21secs. I was up with the leaders for long spells, but I was injured.

Seven members ran from Gloucester AC, and a great weekend was had by all who entered. Martin only lost out on 1st position by a mere 32 seconds.

Our last race in Rosyth was a joyous occasion, but it was rather sad driving back to Gloucester knowing it was for the last time! However, we had just heard that we were being invited to another big race abroad…The European 100km Road Racing Championships in Winschoten, Holland, 11 September 1982. We were hoping it would turn out better than our near disastrous last race in Paris, France.

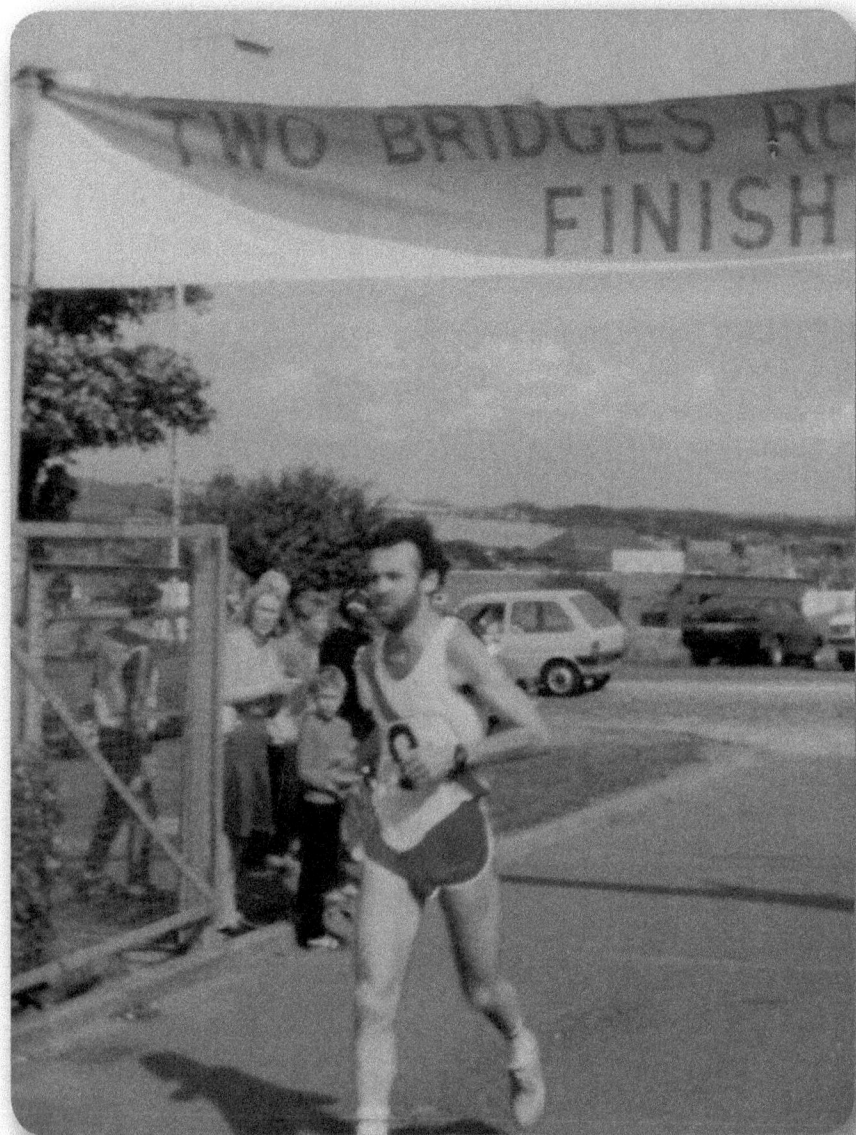

John Conlan finishing in 31st place, B Team
Winner (a new Glos AC member)

Glos AC Martin Daykin, individual
2nd A Team Winner

FUNDRAISING FOR CHARITY

We still found time to have a go at anything else running-related that we could, before major events!

The 'Bed Race'

One of our hardest fun races for charity! It wasn't a bad time either, finishing in a time of 54mins 43secs! We flew around; Dave and Ken never ran so fast, hanging on for dear life, to set PBs.

Another charity race we did was our most gruelling race yet… in the Royal Forest of Dean. It was a 10-mile sponsored 'Chair Race', over hills from Coleford, Speech House to Mitcheldean, in aid of Mitcheldean Charities Organisation.

Gloucester Athletic Club with "The Bullet' on the way to victory in the bed race.

ATHLETES PROVE THEIR FITNESS

GLOUCESTER Athletic Club members proved their fitness when they earned the winner's honours at a major charity bed race yesterday.

Chris O'Carroll, the team captain, was presented with a race trophy after his side crossed the winning line after just 54 minutes, 43 seconds.

Their entry, "The Bullet," was watched by a crowd of 3,000 during the races at the Gloucester Trading Estate.

The bed race, held for the third year in succession, was organised by the South Cotswold and Stonehouse Round table and was expected to raise over £5,000 for charities.

Stroud Sheltered Workshop, based at Stonehouse, and the Cancer and Leukaemia in Childhood Trust will be the main beneficiaries.

The Gloucester bed was closely followed by Stroud and District Athletic Club entry, named "Frapies Flyer."

The fancy dress section was won by Dowty Electrics "Pompeii Palace". "Peacock Punk" were the popular winners of the prize for the side that gave the best entertainment value.

Other successful teams were from Severn Valley Enterprises (five pushers or under); Stroud Athletic Club (6/7 pushers); North Glos. Motorcycle Club (over 7 pushers); Pressweld (Mixed team); Eastcombe Ladies (all female); and Eastcombe Slay (junior team).

A competition for a portable television was won by Mrs. Joan Yewdall from Eastcombe, who donated her prize to Ward 9 at Gloucestershire Royal Hospital.

The Round Table, who were delighted by the tremendous effort and enthusiasm for the event, are looking forward to arranging another event again next year.

We were in an eight-man team from Gloucester AC.

As you can see from the photos, it was a real killer… mentally and physically! A real test. We managed to win it, but we couldn't pick up a pint of beer with either arm for several days. Our backs ached and our legs ached; you name it, we felt it! Although it was a fun day and another win, we wouldn't be doing another race like that ever again!

Back to our next major race now, the European 100km Championships. Bring it on!

R A C E   1 0

(International four-man team contest)
Another big event for the squad!

EUROPEAN 100KM ROAD RACING CHAMPIONSHIPS – 11 SEPTEMBER 1982

Prior to this race, Chris O'Carroll (Glos AC) had approached the AAA hierarchy in London to ask their permission to enter an England representative team, consisting of M. Daykin, M. Pickard, C. Woodward, M.Newton and T. O'Reilly. As was expected, his request was rejected with the reply that there is not enough national participation in the sport of ultra-distance running, or at least no proof of it. But even if proof was forthcoming, then club secretaries and area representatives would have to state this and vote for this type of sport to be recognised to warrant international selection for future events. So any world-class British ultra-distance runners in the present climate cannot run for his or her country in ultra-type races, unless pressure can be exerted by club members on their secretaries to exert further pressure at area level to get the AAAs to change their present thinking on this fast-growing, popular sport. So it looks like the beginning of an uphill struggle to get the international recognition these ultra-distance athletes deserve.

Undeterred by this setback, the Gloucester AC ultra-distance team of Dave Dowdle, Ken Leyshon, Chris O'Carroll and Martin Daykin travelled to Holland to run. As they were the only English runners there, they also ran unofficially as the England team! With a record 138 runners from several European countries, the race started at 5 am on the Saturday morning in very humid conditions.

135

⊃ 20KM

Martin Daykin was disputing the lead with Jan Szumiec (Poland), both going through in 1:17:03; Henk Bronswijk was in 3rd position in 1:17:05, close behind. The Gloucester trio (Leyshon, Dowdle, O'Carroll) all went through in 1:26:05.

⊃ 40KM

Daykin and the Pole Szumiec were still together in 2:33:03 with Bronswijk (Holland) still 3rd in 2:28:05. Bozanich (USA) was in 4th with Henrichs of W. Germany 2:41:04. No more changes occurred down the field, with the Gloucester trio all through in 2:50:02.

⊃ 50KM

The halfway mark of this two-lap race with the weather getting hotter. The team race at this point was between W. Germany and Holland (four to score), W. Germany having eight runners in the first fifteen to Holland's six. Dayton had at last broken clear of the field by 1 minute, clocking 3:13.03. His relentless pace (sub 40mins for every 10km split) began to pay dividends as the rest of the field couldn't stay with him in the hot, humid conditions.

⊃ 60KM

Daykin's lead had now stretched to 4 minutes over Szumiec, 3:53:02 to 3:57:03. Bronswijk was 3rd and Bozanich 4th. Meanwhile, down the field, things had begun to happen. Dowdle and O'Carroll were picking up the pace and were relentlessly going past runner after runner. By the 60km mark, they had both moved up into 8th and 9th positions, both through in 4:13:03. Ken Leyshon had moved up into 16th position and so the team race was wide open, developing into a three-horse race between England, W. Germany and Holland!

⊃ 70KM

Daykin was 6 minutes clear in 4:34.02 from Bronswijk with Kleu (W. Germany) in 3rd. Dowdle and O'Carroll were still 8th and 9th in 4:55:04 but closing on the leaders all the time. Leyshon was up into 12th position 5:01:0.

Ever had that feeling you're being followed?

➲ 80KM

Daykin (5:15.0) held an 8-minute lead over Kleu and Bronswijk, who were both battling it out for 2nd place. Frank Bozanich was in 4th position but closing up all the time. Then came Dowdle and O'Carroll in 5th and 6th positions, bringing the England team right into contention for the team title. Both ran personal bests, clocking 5:38:0. Leyshon was still hanging onto 12th position, 5:55:0.

➲ 90KM

It began to get really hot and runners began to suffer. But the Gloucester lads, knowing they had the team title within their grasp, were really digging in and consolidating their positions.

Daykin was still running away from the field, extending his lead to 10 minutes in 5:56:05 from Kleu (6:06:03) and Bronswijk (6:08:05). Dowdle had caught a tired-looking Bozanich and was in 4th place with O'Carroll 6th. Leyshon was still doggedly hanging onto 12th spot in 6:57:04.

➲ 100KM

Daykin ended up a clear winner by over 12 minutes in 6:39:08. Another great run by this man who is almost unbeatable over the 100km distance; this was his third successive victory in this race. Although nowhere near his record time for the course, it was still a brilliant run considering the hot, humid conditions.

Fourth was Dave Dowdle with a fine 7:05:01. This was his first really good run since his world record 24hr track race last May. Fifth was Frank Bozanich in 7:05:53 and 6th went to Horst Vybiral (W. Germany) in 7:10:43.

Seventh was Gloucester's and England's third man, Chris O'Carroll, in 7:12:40, knocking 35 minutes off his personal best for the distance.

So, with three men home, attention focussed on the fourth Gloucester runner, Ken Leyshon. Ken, although suffering from the heat, hung onto his 12th position, clocking a personal best (by 45 minutes) 7:47:57. This run finally secured Gloucester AC England the team title.

RESULTS

1.	M. Daykin – Glos AC, England	6:39:08
2.	H.W. Kleu – Kerpin AC, W. Germany	6:51:17
3.	H. Bronswijk – Olympus 70, Holland	6:55:04
4.	D. Dowdle – Glos AC, England	7:05:01
5.	F. Bozanich – Univ. Wash. AC, USA	7:05:53
6.	H. Vybiral Haz Bertlich – W. Germany	7:10:42
7.	C. O'Carroll – Glos AC, England	7:12:40
8.	G. Henrichs – TV Salchendorf, W. Germany	7:30:35
9.	W. Scheerenbeck – LAC Marl CV, W. Germany	7:41:36
10.	B. Holstiege Spirdon – Frankfurt, W. Germany	7:42:21
11.	11. J. Szumiec – Polmo, Poland	7:45:24
12.	12. K. Leyshon – Glos AC, England	7:47:57

Team Result (based on average time of four scoring runners)

1. England 7:11:12
2. W. Germany 7:18:32
3. Holland 7:39:03
4. Poland
5. Belgium

(Team result, UK rules!) Close, hey! England 1+4+7+12 = 24 points
Germany 2+6+8+9 = 25 points
Holland 3+14+15+16 = 48 points

Afterwards, at the presentation, the organisers referred to the team winners as the Gloucester Flying Squad, whose reputation they had heard about and now watched firsthand as they relentlessly destroyed a top-class field to win this first-ever European 100km Road Championship.

It was a tremendous run by the Gloucester lads, and thanks are due to the Dutch cyclists who acted as back-up teams and supported the Gloucester squad throughout, carrying all the spare kit and vital drinks on a fast flat course with not much shelter from a hot sun.

139

It was a pity that more English runners didn't run in the race. The race is probably one of the best organised and finest 100km races in Europe. Still, the four Gloucester runners kept up the great tradition of British ultra-distance running, with Frank Bozanich going back home to the States muttering, "Nothing quite like these Gloucester boys at home."

I must also personally thank our Dutch hosts, who looked after all the Gloucester lads, from start to finish!

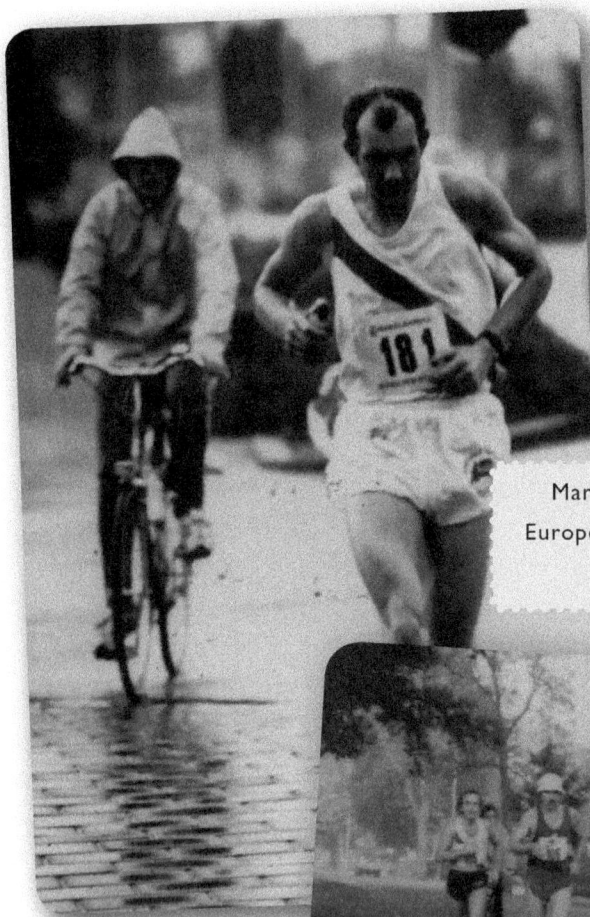

Martin and Dave competing in European 100km Championships in Winschoten, Holland!

GLOS AC TEAM
EUROPEAN CHAMPIONS (UNOFFICIALLY)
FOR YOU
STATSIONS PEOPLE

uitslagen 100 km Run 82 te Winschoten – Ergebnisliste 100 km Run 82 in Winschoten, Holland – Results 100 km Run 82 in Winschoten, Holland

Organisatie – Organisation – Organization Stichting Run Winschoten, Postbus 275, 9670 AG Winschoten, Nederland

start nr.	Aank nr.	Klasse-ment	nr	Naam-Name-Name	Vereniging-Verein-Club	Land	10 km	20 km	30 km	40 km	marat	50 km	60 km	70 km	80 km	90 km	100 km
18	1	S	1	Martin John Daykin	Gloucester AC ※	GB		1.17.3	1.55.0	2.33.3	2.42.4	3.13.3	3.53.2	4.34.2	5.15.0	5.56.5	6.39.08
50	2	V1	1	Hans Werwer Kleu	LAC Kerpen CV	BRD		1.20.4	2.01.5	2.42.0	2.51.3	3.23.1	4.02.3	4.42.2	5.23.0	6.06.3	6.51.17
18	3	S	2	Henk Bronsvijk	Olympus 70	Ned		1.20.1	1.59.4	2.38.5	2.48.2	3.19.2	3.59.3	4.41.0	5.23.0	6.08.5	6.55.04
05	4	S	3	Dave M. Dowdie	Gloucester AC ※	GB		1.26.5	2.09.0	2.50.2	3.00.5	3.31.5	4.13.3	4.55.4	5.33.0	6.20.5	7.05.01
23	5	S	4	Frank Bozanich	Univ of Wash Police	USA		1.21.4	2.01.5	2.41.4	2.51.3	3.23.0	4.03.4	4.47.0	5.33.0	6.20.5	7.05.53
149	6	V1	2	Horst Vybiral	LG Haz Bertlich	BRD		1.21.5	2.00.1	2.40.0	2.49.3	3.22.1	4.05.4	4.50.3	5.38.0	6.23.1	7.10.42
106	7	S	5	Christ O Carroll	Gloucester AC ※	GB		1.27.0	2.09.0	2.50.2	2.59.3	3.31.5	4.13.3	4.55.4	5.38.0	6.21.3	7.12.40
100	8	S	6	Gerd Henrichs	TV Salchendorf	BRD		1.21.0	2.00.5	2.41.4	2.50.0	3.27.0	4.11.3	4.58.4	5.48.0	6.39.5	7.30.35
112	9	S	7	Werner Scheerenbeck	LAC Marl Cv	BRD		1.20.4	2.00.1	2.40.0	2.49.3	3.22.2	4.05.4	4.50.3	5.55.0	6.47.2	7.41.36
164	10	V1	3	Bernd Holstiege	Spiridon Frankfurt	BRD		1.25.0	2.10.5	2.55.3	3.05.2	3.40.1	4.24.1	5.09.1	6.00.5	6.47.1	7.42.21
13	11	S	8	Jan Szuniec	Polmo	Pol		1.17.3	1.55.0	2.33.3	2.42.4	3.14.1	3.57.4	4.50.5	5.52.0	6.50.1	7.45.24
107	12	S	9	Kenneth A. Leyshon	Gloucester AC ※	GB		1.27.4	2.09.0	2.50.2	3.00.1	3.31.5	4.15.1	5.01.5	5.55.0	6.57.4	7.47.57
154	13	V1	4	Heinz G. Schmidt	LC Stolpertruppe ※	BRD		1.20.0	1.58.5	2.40.4	2.51.1	3.24.4	4.16.0	5.05.1	6.01.0	6.55.4	7.48.00
79	14	V2	1	David Markwick	AV Te Werve	Ned		1.23.3	2.03.3	2.43.1	2.52.5	3.24.4	4.09.0	4.58.2	6.06.4	6.57.4	7.48.13
60	15	S	5	Siem Deen		Ned		1.32.1	2.17.1	3.02.5	3.13.1	3.48.1	4.32.3	5.17.3	6.04.5	6.58.3	7.53.10
13	16	S	10	Henk Loots	Aquilo	Ned		1.34.3	2.22.2	3.10.1	3.21.1	3.56.4	4.41.0	5.30.5	6.19.0	7.08.4	7.59.47
48	17	V1	6	Aleksander Stojadinovil	LAZ Berg Gladbach	BRD		1.29.2	2.13.0	2.58.5	3.09.42	3.46.0	4.34.1	5.29.5	6.23.0	7.16.1	8.04.48
47	18	V1	7	Anton M. Stam	Vet Ned Apeldoorn	Ned		1.30.0	2.14.4	3.00.0	3.10.4	3.47.0	4.33.2	5.27.0	6.17.0	7.09.4	8.07.41
145	19	V1	8	Dietrich Tiem	TUS Holstein Quickborn	BRD		1.30.0	2.14.4	2.59.1	3.09.5	3.46.1	4.34.3	5.22.5	6.15.0	7.11.0	8.09.54
21	20	S	11	Jan Jongste	Vet Ned Apeldoorn	Ned		1.38.4	2.29.1	3.18.5	3.30.3	4.08.3	4.56.1	5.47.1	6.37.0	7.31.4	8.23.59
49	21	S	9	Derk J v.d. Laan	Aquilo	Ned		1.42.1	2.04.1	2.47.4	2.57.5	3.33.2	4.22.2	5.15.2	6.15.0	7.20.2	8.26.02
7	22	S	12	Harry van Dijk	AV Oss 78	Ned		1.36.5	2.24.1	3.10.3	3.21.5	4.00.0	4.46.3	5.45.3	6.42.0	7.39.1	8.32.46
55	23	S	10	Jan Lacaeyse	Sobek-Zwevegen	B		1.38.4	2.29.1	3.17.0	3.29.0	4.14.1	5.01.2	5.51.3	6.44.0	7.39.3	8.36.00
41	24	V1	11	Kees Oosterling	AV Veluwe Apeldoorn	Ned		1.34.2	2.22.2	3.11.1	3.22.5	4.03.5	4.57.1	5.52.0	6.47.0	7.41.5	8.36.42
11	25	V1	13	Josef Kaderhandt	Letmathet TV	BRD		1.35.1	2.22.2	3.09.4	3.21.0	3.59.0	4.47.3	5.38.4	6.33.0	7.29.1	8.37.18
16	26	S	14	Henryk Czerniak	Tonsil	Pol		1.37.1	2.25.2	3.14.4	3.26.0	4.03.4	4.54.1	5.48.3	6.47.0	7.45.5	8.40.27
5	27	S	15	Gerard Klein	NEA Volharding	Ned		1.38.0	2.28.2	3.17.2	3.28.5	4.06.3	4.58.1	5.51.5	6.58.0	7.58.1	8.50.38
61	28	V1	12	Rob Brouwer	Vet Ned Apeldoorn	Ned		1.38.4	2.28.3	3.18.5	3.30.3	4.08.3	4.56.1	5.47.4	6.50.2	7.52.2	8.51.44
157	29	V1	13	Gerhard Werner	LG Baaberg	BRD		1.41.2	2.28.2	3.14.3	3.25.4	4.02.2	4.56.1	5.55.0	6.57.0	7.56.5	8.53.22
16	30	S	16	Ben Hagen	NSL Noordwijkerhout	Ned		1.28.5	2.14.1	3.00.0	3.10.5	3.50.3	4.43.3	5.43.4	6.46.0	7.50.5	8.55.31
125	31	S	17	Detlef Ruppel	LV Stolpertruppe	BRD		1.45.0	2.36.0	3.29.2	3.41.3	4.20.4	5.12.4	6.08.5	7.07.0	8.05.2	8.57.15
6	32	S	18	Simon Klein	Vet Ned Apeldoorn	Ned		1.28.0	2.13.4	3.00.0	3.10.5	3.48.4	4.38.0	5.33.5	6.40.0	7.53.3	8.59.01
174	33	V2	2	Gunther Weiss	SC Glashutten	BRD		1.42.0	2.32.0	3.25.0	3.38.0	4.19.1	5.14.1	6.12.3	7.12.0	8.11.5	9.11.43
48	34	V1	14	Aldert Groen	Vet Ned Apeldoorn	Ned		1.27.2	2.09.4	2.52.3	3.02.2	3.44.2	4.46.0	5.49.4	6.48.0	7.56.5	9.14.31
10	35	S	19	Henk Noor	Aquilo	Ned		1.17.5	1.59.1	2.45.0	2.56.0	3.48.1	4.44.0	5.46.0	6.51.0	7.55.5	9.15.11
74	36	V2	3	Jan Wielens	Vet Ned Apeldoorn	Ned		1.47.0	2.40.4	3.32.4	3.45.1	4.26.2	5.22.5	6.17.5	7.25.0	8.24.0	9.19.38

1ST TEAM GB 24 PTS 2ND TEAM GERMANY 25 PTS

Uit slagen 100 km Run 82 te Winschoten - Ergebnisliste 100 km Run 82 in Winschoten, Holland - Results 100 km Run 82 in Winschoten, Holland

Organisatie - Organisation - Organization Stichting Run Winschoten, Postbus 275, 9670 AG Winschoten, Nederland

Start nr.	Aank nr.	Klassement	Naam-Name-Name	Vereniging-Verein-Club	Land	10 km	20 km	30 km	40 km	marat	50 km	60 km	70 km	80 km	90 km	100 km
3	73	S 32	Ron de Boer	Pers.lid KNAU	Ned		1.38.2	2.28.0	3.21.2	3.35.1	4.21.3	5.33.0	7.06.4	8.35.0	10.00.4	11.22.46
22	74	S 33	Joost Timmermans	A dam AU Club	Ned		2.04.1	2.57.4	3.53.3	4.06.3	4.51.1	5.51.1	6.58.1	9.13.0	10.21.2	11.24.28
45	75	V1 28	Cor v.d. Kooy	Vet Ned Apeldoorn	Ned		1.47.4	2.44.3	3.42.4	3.58.2	4.53.0	6.17.1	7.33.3	9.00.0	10.26.3	11.51.25
75	76	V2 12	F. Koenes	Vet Ned Apeldoorn	Ned		1.58.2	2.57.3	4.02.1	4.16.5	5.09.4	6.28.4	7.50.0	9.11.0	10.33.1	11.53.30
146	77	V1 29	Adolf Reimers	TUS Wesseling	BRD		1.53.1	2.58.0	4.06.2	4.27.2	5.24.0	6.35.3	8.01.3	9.23.0	10.46.4	12.03.08
77	78	V2 13	H. Doornekamp	Altis Amersfoort	Ned		1.47.1	2.43.4	3.45.0	3.57.1	5.07.1	6.25.0	7.55.1	9.22.0	10.48.5	12.14.12
51	79	V1 30	Bauke te Nyenhuis	Vet Ned Apeldoorn	Ned		2.19.3	3.26.0	4.35.4	4.51.5	5.48.1	7.10.4	8.29.1	9.44.0	10.55.5	12.32.18
57	80	V1 31	Johannes P. de Mooy	AV De Keien	Ned		1.44.1	2.40.5	3.44.5	4.00.4	5.23.0	6.38.1	8.08.1	9.44.0	11.00.0	12.33.48
4	81	S 34	Fred van Bruchem	GAC Hilversum	Ned		1.49.4	2.45.4	3.45.3	4.00.1	5.06.3	6.27.0	8.10.4	9.34.0	11.00.0	12.34.09
102			Nick Wendel	TUS Halver 1848 CV	BRD		1.31.0	2.19.0	3.07.1	3.20.0	3.57.4	4.48.2	5.52.4			
151			Siegfried Wachhaus	LG Wilhelmshaven	BRD		1.29.2	2.14.1	2.59.5	3.09.5		4.34.2	5.26.2			
62			Jan te Brake	Ava 70 Aalten	Ned		1.46.3	2.40.4	3.32.4	3.45.1	4.25.4	5.16.2	6.45.3			
141			Hans Rosenberger	SV Rosselshousen	BRD		1.21.3	2.07.1	2.43.2	3.05.2	3.46.5	4.38.4				
101			Rogiers Noel	AC Meetjesland	B		1.38.5	2.28.1	3.17.0	3.29.0	4.10.4	5.08.1				
153			Marian Kobiela	Polno	Pol		1.59.2	3.04.5	4.20.2	4.37.3	5.40.4	7.10.4				
8			J.W. Dijkgraaf	SV De Lat Leeuwarden	Ned		2.19.0	3.24.0	4.32.5	4.48.5	5.46.1	7.11.5				
162			Eero Mahitalo	SC Glashutten	BRD		1.36.4	2.25.1	3.16.4	3.29.0	4.12.1	5.13.2				
108			Hans Henri Timmermann	LAZ Main Kinaig Habau	BRD			2.10.5	2.54.5	3.06.0	3.42.2					
9			Frank Bouwhuis	Aquilo	B		1.38.1	2.27.5	3.21.4	3.34.5						
127			Lucien van Lancker	Kasvoudenaarde	B		1.22.1	2.04.0	2.46.2	2.56.2	3.30.3					
1			Hans Wikkers	AV Castricum	Ned		1.22.2	2.02.3	2.51.3	3.02.4						
11			Johan Hulsebos	Aquilo	Ned		1.46.3	2.39.0	3.35.1	3.54.0						
59			Drees Aalten	Arena Athl. Rhemen	Ned		1.44.1	2.35.0	3.31.3	3.48.3						
72			Henk v Damme	Impala Drachten	Ned		1.46.1	2.46.4	3.53.4	4.10.3						
76			H. Rood	Vet Ned Apeldoorn	Ned		1.34.4	2.25.4	3.19.0	3.30.4						
80			Paul NaumANN	Vet Ned Apeldoorn	Ned		1.46.1	2.40.4	3.42.5	3.59.0						
115			Jerzy Kotelecki	Polma	Pol		1.26.5	2.12.1	3.03.1	3.14.3						
129			Hubert Lacroix	Chaudfontain	B		2.12.5	3.43.0	5.15.2	5.38.0						
142			Fernand Tonneau	KASV Ouder arde	B		1.26.4	2.08.3								
130			Jean Fr Delasalle	Amiens Un Club	Fr		2.02.3									

Martin competing in European 100km Championships in Winschoten, Holland!

1st, Martin: What can you say about this man! A legend in his own right! Almost unbeatable at 100km races and world class on all ultra distances from 50km up to 200km. (insert photo for each runner)

4th, Dave: Another ultra legend and world-class record-holder! On the day, a virtual machine who never stops, whatever the distance!

7th, Chris: Who always slots in somewhere! Keeps setting personal bests as he moves up into the world class at ultra distances! Another unstoppable team member!

12th, Ken: Had brought his eldest daughter Sonia with him, who accompanied him on a bicycle the whole way! Keeping him well hydrated throughout! Personal best for Ken by 45 minutes! Vital team-run to secure the team victory, great run!

Make no mistake, this was a brutal race! We ran over two laps in very hot conditions, with no shade or cover! It was constantly getting hotter and hotter! 138 runners started the race, from several countries! Only 45 runners finished, 93 runners didn't finish!

With people on bikes accompanying the runners with their drinks during the race, the whole Gloucester squad were drinking every 15-20 minutes throughout, right from the start! If you hit the wall in one of these ultra-distance races, you're gone! No comeback or you lose too much time! This is why on long training runs at home we don't take any drinks during the run itself. When a lot of ultra runners take drinks with them all the time. The body greedily absorbs the energy very quickly, because it thinks there won't be another for a long time. There will probably be some arguments about this method of training for distance running, but as you can see from our results, it certainly proved helpful.

We ended the race in a head-to-head fight against the Germans! All the way to the finish; there were seconds and minutes in the stand we didn't even know where the Gloucester squad had finished, until the final results were announced! It was physically and mentally one of our hardest races yet on the road.

So the Gloucester squad were now (unofficially) **100km European Team Champions 1982**. It was a very tired but happy group of Gloucester athletes and supporters who drove back to the UK.

Footnote

At the Dutch border, customs officials stopped the cars and ordered Martin out to take photos with him! They had seen the 100km race in the Dutch press and TV, which was fantastic! We were all literally waved through customs, with a boot full of *liqueur*… I mean, goodies. Onwards and upwards; it was going to be hard to top this whole occasion, as it was our biggest win as a team to date!

Martin Daykin, one of England's greatest exponents of 100km races, winning races all over Europe. A legend in UK, France, Holland, Germany, Finland in Ultra Distance Running.

Setting the pace in Holland

Martin wooing the crowds in
Santander, Spain

RACE 11

‖ First race of its kind in the UK! ‖

After our successful 100km race in Holland, it was back to Gloucester AC Winter Cross-Country fixture lists for 1982/1983, competing also in Gloucester Club road races in 1983.

No major ultra-distance races on the horizon, but there was a 24-hour 4-man relay race, around the athletic track (which had never been done in the UK before). I don't know whose idea it was, or who got interested in it, but it was an attempt to go for another world record; so we were off again. The current world record was set by the White Track Club, in Kentucky, USA, with a distance of 234 miles ran in 1979. Interest began to grow around our event and a plan began to formulate.

The date, time and venue were discussed and agreed with Cheltenham Harriers, and below are the official details.

GLOUCESTER ATHLETIC CLUB
proudly present
FIRST TIME EVER IN THE U.K.

24
HOUR

FOUR
MAN

RELAY
RACE

(Held under RRC/AAA Rules)
in aid of

Crack Cancer Campaign

Breast Cancer Treatment Machine for the Cobalt Unit, Cheltenham General
Hospital to treat patients throughout the South West.

Venue
Prince of Wales Stadium, Tommy Taylors Lane,
Cheltenham Town

Saturday, 2nd April, 1983   6 pm Start
Admission by Programme   40p
KEEP YOUR PROGRAMME
Lucky Prize Draw/Programme Number

RULES

1. Before starting each team must declare the order the members will run in.

2. This order must be kept throughout the race.

3. If a runner misses his turn to run he may not run again. The team may continue.

4. Each runner must run 4 complete laps. Incomplete legs will not count. Multiples of 4 laps are not allowed.

5. The team may stop to rest if it so decides.

6. The team manager is responsible for ensuring runners are ready at the take-over point.

7. A Baton must be carried by each team for the duration of the race. It must be exchanged within the takeover box.

7. All warming up must take place outside the track or on the back straight.

-2-

149

OFFICIALS

Race Secretary	C. O'Carroll
Race Managers	A. Daley
	S. Daley
Chief Timekeeper	A. Birt
Asst. Timekeeper	B. Hussey
Physiotherapist	Mrs. Griffiths

The Committee of Gloucester Athletic Club
are grateful for the help provided by:-

BOURTON ROAD RUNNERS AC
GLOUC ATH CLUB
CHELTENHAM HARRIERS AC

and many individuals not members of Gloucester
Athletic Club for their invaluable assistance
in lap recording.

The Committee extend their grateful thanks to

Mr. Smith and Mr. Lawrence

and the Stadium Ground Staff for their
assistance in promoting this event.

-7-

150

BREAST CANCER — A NEW TOMORROW

CANCER * CHALLENGE * COBALT — all words beginning
with a 'Big C' epitomising the matchless story
of the Appeal Fund which founded, funded and
ceaselessly supports the Cancer Treatment and
Research Centre at Cheltenham.

And now the Appeal faces its greatest challenge
yet — for a Breast Cancer Treatment Machine.
The total cost of the project of £1,000,000 is
being met in equal partnership with the National
Health Service.

Breast cancer is the most common form of cancer
in women — one in twenty contract it.

Now it has been proved that in many cases this
disease can be controlled by an alternative
treatment to disfiguring surgery.

"There is much to do in the months to come but
our aim is to be ready to treat patients by the
summer of 1984" said Dr. Fred Hanna, Chairman of
the Cobalt Appeal Fund. "The treatment machine,
once commissioned, will be fully occupied."

"Early diagnosis is essential and we must get the
message to all women that they need no longer
fear that surgery is the only answer to breast
cancer. With this realisation we sincerely hope
that if they suspect anything is wrong, they will
immediately go for examination."

I should like to record my own and my committee's
thanks to the Gloucester Athletic Club for linking
our Campaign to this attack on the world 24 hour
Track Relay Record, and to wish all participants
in the race every success.

-1- Allan Roseberry

151

TEAMS THAT LINED UP FOR THIS EVENT

TEAMS

Cheltenham Flyers   COMPOSITE TEAM   GLOS B TEAM

Ken Buckle   PAUL COLLINS   DF
Dave Rudman   KEN SHAW
Richard Thornton
Dave Dowdle DNF.

Glos. A (white vest red diagonal right to left)

Chris O'Carroll
Martin Daykin
Ken Leyshon
Stan Dalby

100km. Assoc. Team

Malcolm Campbell
Bruce Slade
Ken Shaw
Roger Lawton

Severn Vale Ladies

Tina McCauley   Anne Other
Shani Griffiths   Ann Other

Tipton (green hoops on white)

Bill Carr
Alan Eversin
Colin Hunt
Ron Bentley

South London Harriers (white vest, maroon shorts)

A Team
Charlie Hunn
Arthur Johns
Paul Rafferty
John Watkins

B Team
Mike Gidley
Brian Over
Dave Parkinson
Alec Randle

Hillington A.C. (white vest, red diagonal left to right)

A Team
Vic Gutteridge
Z. Grayson
A. McFadyen
P. Barry

B Team
E.Gutteridge 0/40
M.Casse   0/40
M.Miller   0/40
D.Blackett   0/40

Cheltenham and County Harriers (white vest 2 black hoops)

Dave McNamee
Shaun Colvin
Bob Hamilton
Brian Heaford

Back to the hills training again. Most of these runs were 10 miles+ at 6 in the morning, bearing in mind we also had full-time jobs, although a lot of our overseas competitors thought we were all full-time professionals.

Our second run of the day was in the evenings, running 16miles+. I worked in computers for Walls Ice cream on a shift system, which in winter allowed me to train earlier in the evenings.

This race, though, presented us with a total change of training and tactics! From March (with cross-country season finished), we started to wind down the high mileage and start to concentrate on speed work… which also worked out well for the relay season in the UK.

I started running track work at faster than race pace. One session would be 16 x 220 at sub 35 second pace x 16. 1 mile warm up, 1 mile warm down, with a 220 recovery. This would be sub 4 minutes 40 seconds pace! I found this session ideal three times a week. (My PB 10-mile time: 50 minutes.)

If you want to set PBs, whatever they are, always train shorter distances faster than your PB times. An ideal distance is 200m as it is easy to recover after the session. Also, the recovery run must be accurate. If you're too slow, there will be no benefit, and going too fast might mean you won't get through the session at speed. Wearing a heart rate monitor will help you to control the recovery heart rate correctly, before the efforts again. Remember, the recovery is more important than the run! You can vary the distances to suit, 200m to 100m; remember the recovery rate before you go again. Hope that might be of some help to you budding runners out there, whatever distances you run!

The relay race soon started to get nearer, with all four of us sharpening up. This race seemed to be easier; four laps each looked a doddle, but we would soon come to regret this line of thought, as you'll come to find out shortly.

As said earlier in the book, all our distances in training were faster than our PB times over a 100km distance. My own 100km PB was 7hrs 12mins. I trained most distance runs faster than my PB time for 100km. 16km runs in 60/65 minutes pace! Some of our Sunday runs were marathon distance, in 2 hours 35 minutes/2 hours 45 minutes approximately. So whatever your PB, on the track or road, remember, train shorter distances faster than your PB pace. Use a heart rate monitor to recover your heart rate at your normal recovery rate, before doing another effort.

So the race story enfolded thus…

(As said earlier in the book, no drinks were taken with us on our training runs… whatever the distance.)

Chris O'Carroll
Anchorman

The first-ever 24-hour four-man relay took place on April 2nd/3rd at the Prince of Wales Stadium in Cheltenham. Eight teams lined up for the event but, due to injuries and non-arrivals, two teams ran with only three men: the South London Harriers 'A' team and the 100km Association team. The complete line-up was as follows:

⊃ FOUR-MAN TEAMS

Gloucester AC 'A' team – Martin Daykin, Chris O'Carroll, Stan Dalby and Ken Leyshon
Cheltenham AC – Ken Buckle, Bob Hamilton, Brian Heaford and Dave Rudman
Hillingdon AC 'A' team – Vic Gutteridge, Zig Grzywna, Andy McFadyen and Paul Barry
Hillingdon AC 'B' team – Erik Gutteridge (o/40), Mike Casse (o/40), Mike Miller (o/40) and Dave Blackett (o/ 40)
Gloucester AC 'B' team – Ken Shaw, Richard Thornton, Dave Dowdle (using the race as training for the forthcoming 24-hour race in Vienna) and Paul Collins

⊃ THREE-MAN TEAMS

100 km Association – Bruce Slade, Malcolm Campbell and Roger Lawton
South London Harriers 'A' team – Charlie Hunn, Arthur Johns and Brian Owers
South London Harriers 'B' team – Mike Giddey, Alec Randle and Dave Parkinson

At 6.17 pm, the field got away to a cracking start with plenty of records to aim for (the world three-man of 222 1/2 miles set by a West German team and the world four-man of 234 miles set by an American team). The Gloucester 'A' team started particularly fast with O'Carroll running a 4:57 opening mile and Daykin following with a 4:53 of his own. Most of the other teams started a bit more sedately, but after an hour's running, it was, as expected, the Gloucester 'A' team who were in the lead and well up on the sub-6-minute mile schedule required to crack the world best.

The Hillingdon 'A' team were also starting to move into top gear, with Paul Barry and Andy Mcfadyen looking very strong. These two were under record schedule as were the SLH three-man team. The Hillingdon vets' team was also moving very smoothly and, with Arthur and Sheilagh Daley coordinating the lap recorders, everything seemed peaceful and well under control. How quickly this scene was to change!

Around midnight, Mother Nature decided to take a hand and saw fit to unleash freezing temperatures, strong winds, rain, hailstones and eventually when it seemed as though conditions could get no worse, snow. The first people to suffer were the lap recorders, exposed to the elements on trackside and with the burden of trying to record each lap for each competitor accurately. Eventually, as conditions worsened, everything, including the lap recorders, was

Stan Dalby, Glos AC, celebrating going through the world record!

moved into the more sheltered area of the stands. The runners at this stage were just going through the motions, running their required four laps, disappearing and reappearing when they were required once again.

With additional outer garments donned to forestall the effects of the bitter cold, the pace inevitably slackened, although the leading teams were still inside world record pace. At the 12- hour mark, the storms began to abate, and as the dawn broke, Gloucester were still in the lead, having logged 206km/128.75 miles. In 2nd position were Hillingdon 'A' team on 199.6km/124.75 miles, while 3rd were the SLH three-man team on 195.3km/122 miles. Hillingdon 'B' were in 4th, SLH 'B' 5th, Cheltenham 6th, Gloucester 'B' 7th and the 100km Association 8th. Surprisingly, the Hillingdon 'A' team were beginning to hold the leading Gloucester team, and even more surprisingly, the SLH three-man team were still in contention.

As 16 hours was reached, Gloucester began to realise that they had a fight on their hands and were beginning to regret having gone so fast so early. The pace was beginning to take its toll visibly as both Leyshon and O'Carroll started to tire and struggled to maintain 6-minute miling. By way of contrast, Stan Dalby and Martin Daykin were still banging out sub sixes and were having their own private battle to record the faster splits (Daykin averaging 5.34 and Dalby 5.40).

Hillingdon, spotting the trouble that the leaders were having, tried all they could to keep the pressure on and close the gap, but the effort proved too much for them and too late. The 16-hour positions were as follows:

Gloucester 'A' team – 272.4km / 170 miles
Hillingdon 'A' – 264.4km / 165.25 miles
SLH – 257.2km / 160.75 miles Hillingdon vets' team – 250.8 km / 156.75 miles

At 20 hours, the Gloucester lead had increased to 12km over Hillingdon and, although all the leaders were running with renewed determination, Stan Dalby in particular looked especially strong. The Hillingdon 'A' team had one member, Paul Barry, reduced to a crawl, and the Gloucester squad really began to capitalise on this. Vic Gutteridge from Hillingdon was also beginning to feel the pace, although Andy Mcfadyen was performing heroics in keeping his team on course for the world best.

But the heroics were not confined to Hillingdon, as behind them the SLH three-man squad were beginning to pull Hillingdon back and were just 6km behind. The vets' team in 4th spot were setting new records all the way due to the fact that no four-man vets' team is known to have completed this event, and they all seemed to be running the race of their lives.

By the time 22 hours had elapsed, the track had begun to resemble a battlefield as the efforts of the early fast pace and the cold weather forced runner after runner to retire or just hobble around the required four laps. Paul Collins and Dave Dowdle both retired from the Gloucester 'B' team, leaving a rather annoyed Ken Shaw and Richard Thornton to continue. Both runners had been asked to make up this composite team and felt rather let down at being left to finish alone.

Nevertheless, the 23rd hour of competition saw world bests drawing ever nearer. First to enter new territory were the Gloucester squad who cracked the old world best with 22 hours and 21 minutes elapsed. Stan Dalby had the honour of passing the 234-mile mark on his leg and handed over to a much happier Chris O'Carroll.

He carried their baton through the world four-man team-record — and then found that it was his turn to take the 24-hour race to its conclusion. Celebrating with a well-earned collapse, Gloucester's Stan Dalby awaits the arrival of a welcome pint of best bitter.

➲ STATISTICS

Chris, best mile – 4mins 57secs

Martin, best mile – 4mins 48secs

Ken, best mile – 5mins 16secs

Stan, best mile – 5mins 02secs

Average Mile Time for 24hrs

Chris, average – 5mins 47secs

Martin, average – 5mins 32secs

Ken, average – 6mins 12secs

Stan, average – 5mins 38secs

<u>Average mile time for all four runners</u>
<u>5mins 57.66secs</u>

<u>Miles covered 61.64 miles each</u>
<u>x 4 = 246.56 miles</u>

A NEW WORLD RECORD!

CHRIS	MARTIN	KEN	STAN
5 10	* 5 07	5 16	5 22
5 20	* 5 09	5 28	5 39
5 16	* 4 48	5 17	5 02
* 4 57	5 11	5 19	5 25
5 16	* 5 07	5 28	5 32
5 31	* 5 08	5 28	5 21
5 24	* 5 05	5 26	5 43
5 27	* 5 12	5 37	5 28
5 17	* 5 14	5 32	5 32
5 28	* 5 22	5 29	5 28
5 17	* 5 08	5 44	5 25
* 5 17	5 21	5 53	5 35
5 39	5 39	6 01	* 5 26
5 34	5 32	5 42	* 5 24
5 36	* 5 31	5 46	5 37
5 35	* 5 21	5 54	* 5 21
5 34	* 5 27	5 53	5 32
5 39	* 5 26	5 55	5 34
5 29	* 5 27	6 01	5 37
5 47	* 5 34	6 10	5 40
5 48	* 5 31	6 10	* 5 31
5 51	* 5 27	5 55	5 42
5 51	* 5 34	5 51	5 42
5 37	* 5 33	6 01	5 43
5 48	* 5 34	6 02	5 47
5 53	5 38	6 06	* 5 36
5 49	* 5 31	6 09	5 37
5 41	* 5 28	6 07	5 34
5 49	* 5 38	6 10	5 46
5 57	* 5 34	6 06	5 52
5 49	* 5 24	6 05	5 47
6 06	* 5 36	6 03	5 41
5 57	* 5 34	6 05	5 41
5 56	* 5 34	6 10	5 47
6 07	* 5 37	6 12	* 5 37
5 48	* 5 28	6 04	5 40
* 5 24	5 26	6 07	5 44
5 33	* 5 26	6 25	5 48
5 38	* 5 27	6 41	5 39
5 48	* 5 37	6 18	5 49
5 42	* 5 33	6 34	5 43
5 43	* 5 36	6 20	5 41
5 41	5 35	6 26	* 5 27
5 43	5 35	6 26	* 5 34
5 50	* 5 24	6 24	5 43
5 57	* 5 44	6 22	5 50
* 5 39	5 50	6 28	5 53
6 06	* 5 38	6 29	5 57
6 03	* 5 33	6 27	5 42
5 58	5 37	6 26	* 5 34
6 05	* 5 43	6 24	5 52
5 57	5 56	6 31	* 5 38
5 51	5 46	6 44	* 5 31
6 20	5 38	6 39	* 5 26
5 42	* 5 28	6 32	* 5 38
6 23	5 41	6 52	* 5 29
* 5 31	5 36	6 58	5 34
6 05	* 5 39	6 52	5 52
6 06	* 5 34	7 02	5 38
6 36	* 5 46	7 25	6 02
8 06	8 18	8 02	* 6 18
9 26	8 05	8 01	3 58
av. 5:47.65	av. 5:32.76	av. 6:12.10	av. 5:38.16
mile 5:49.68	mile 5:34.70	mile 6:14.27	mile 5:40.13

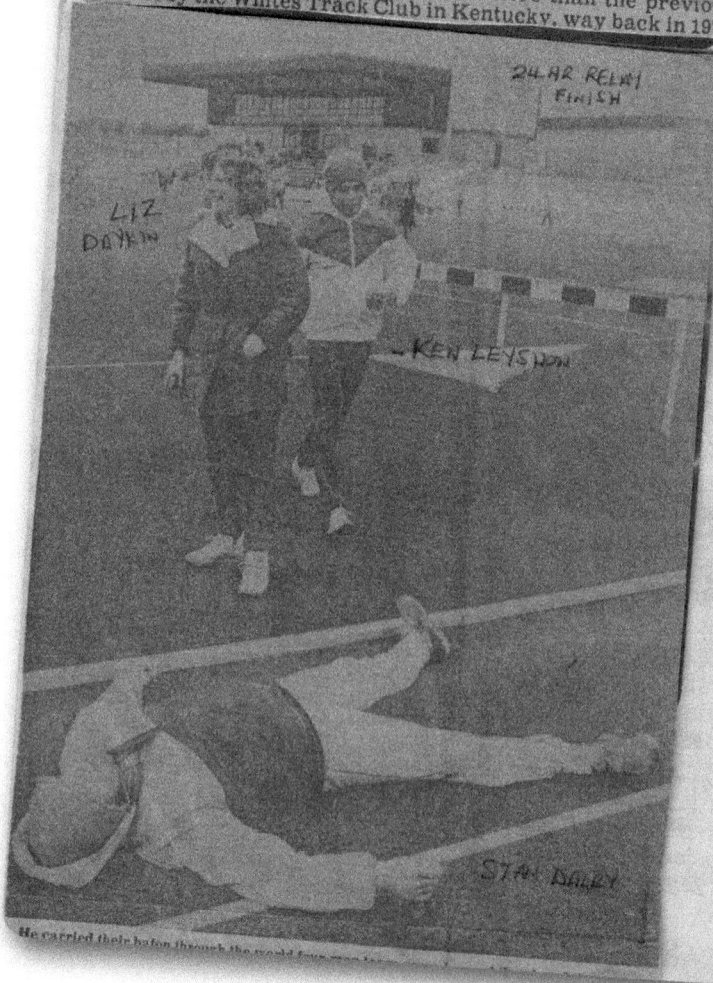

10 Gloucestershire Echo, Monday, April 4, 1983

WORLD RECORD SHATTERED...

Gloucester's four-man team cover 246 miles

IN A GRUELLING test of stamina against the elements, Gloucester Athletic Club's world-beating ultra-distance squad cracked the world record for the four-man 24-hour relay-race at the Prince of Wales Stadium yesterday, writes Timekeeper.

They covered 246 miles — 12 miles more than the previous best set by the Whites Track Club in Kentucky, way back in 1979.

24-HR RELAY FINISH

LIZ DAYKIN

KEN LEYSHON

STAN DAILEY

He carried their baton through the world four-man 24-hour

Martin Daykin, early morning, after arctic conditions overnight

Stan Dalby passing the previous world best! A bit warmer now!

161

WORLD RECORD SHATTERED – GLOUCESTER'S FOUR-MAN TEAM COVER 246 MILES

What we thought was a rather soft world best, turned out to be a tough ordeal! Sprinting off at sub 5mins miles and just over 5min miling, soon lost its appeal as Mother Nature took a hand in proceedings. Rain, wind, hail, snow; you name it, it was thrown at us! Special thanks to new Gloucester AC member Stan Dalby (ex-7th Para Regt), who stepped up to take the place of Dave Dowdle, with distinction.

Must thank all the timekeepers, who had to endure all the weather conditions throughout, and also Arthur and Sheilagh of Gloucester AC who managed the whole race.

Special mention for Bourton Road Runners, led by Norman Lane and his brother. They came to do a stint of lap recordings but ended up staying for the whole 24 hours+. As Norman told me, he couldn't believe the times we were achieving! Most of his runners couldn't run 1 mile much under 6 minutes for one flat-out!

Thanks also to our physiotherapist, Mrs Griffiths, who works like a Trojan to keep us all on the go, throughout the terrible weather. Again, sterling work by Gloucester AC members helping out everywhere!

As pointed out earlier, Dave Dowdle opted out of the Gloucester 'A' team so he could have an easier race in the 'B' team. He wanted to mainly concentrate on the 48-hour track race to be held in Gloucester, Friday 13th/14th May 1983.
Judging by the weather, he made the right choice… we wished him all the best for the 48-hour race!

Our eleventh race, another success, with a world record! Five and a half weeks later, an attack on the 48-hour track world record, of 237miles+, was to be attempted!

R A C E   1 2

Our 12th Major Race (was to be our last together as an ultra-distance squad)

An attempt on the current world record of 381.6km/237.202 miles!

This was to be our last race together as a four-man squad! Our private life circumstances had changed. I had been made redundant from my job at Walls Ice cream, who were moving offices to London. Likewise, Ken Leyshon also had to change jobs. I had been offered the chance to open a retail sports shop in Gloucester (Gloucester Sports), and with a young family to support, my days of gallivanting over Europe were over! I went into partnership with a fellow friend of mine, Tony Wright, who was also made redundant from Walls Ice cream. Tony incidentally cycled over 80 miles with me on my 100-mile race, supporting me with food and drinks along the way (he thought I was slightly mad). Another kindred spirit; I owe him a lot!

Rather sad, but glad it was our last hurrah. I decided not to race but instead made sure the whole event got up and running and I was there to support the runners.

48-HOUR PROGRAMME
13–14 May 1983

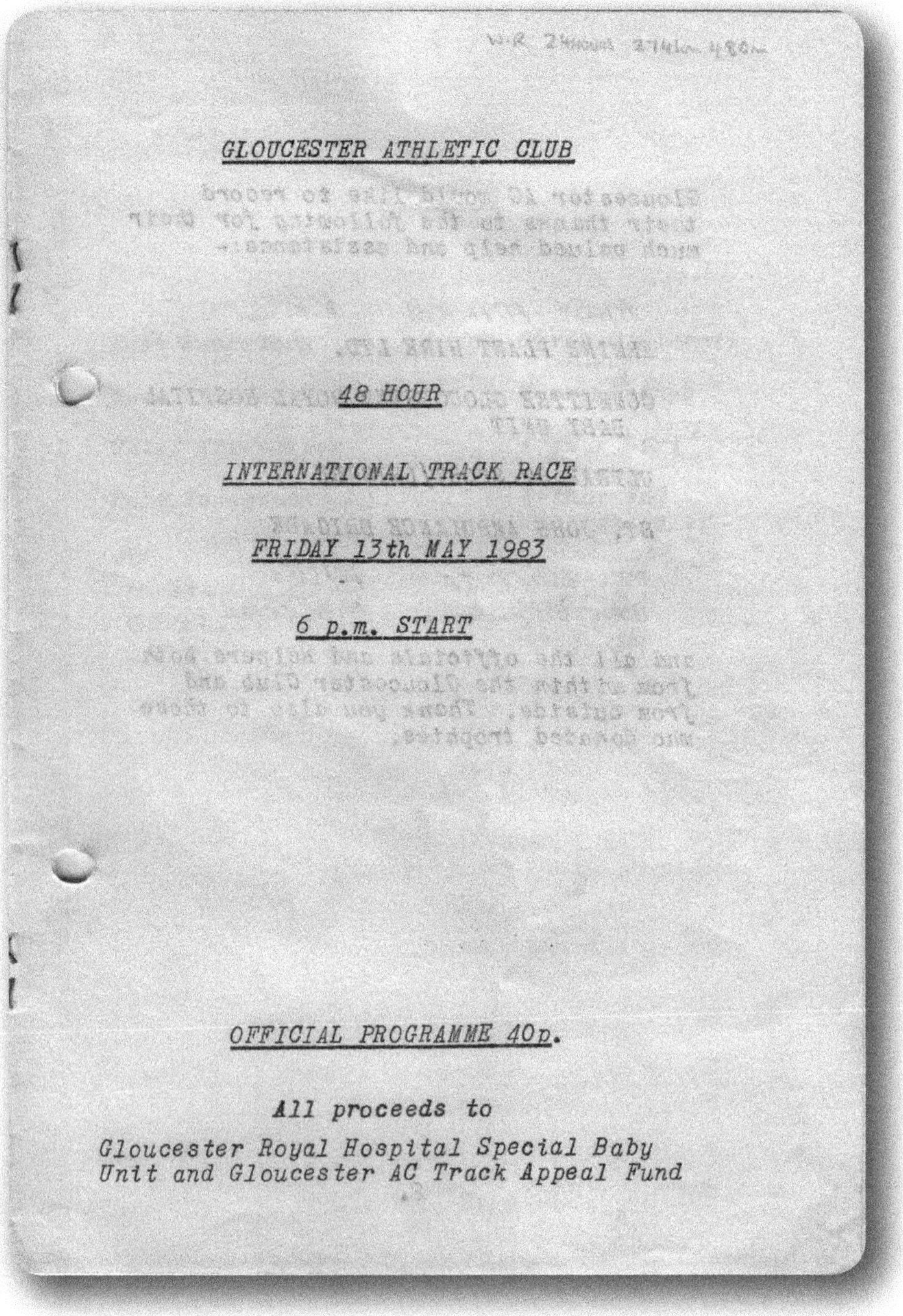

GLOUCESTER ATHLETIC CLUB

48 HOUR

INTERNATIONAL TRACK RACE

FRIDAY 13th MAY 1983

6 p.m. START

OFFICIAL PROGRAMME 40p.

All proceeds to
Gloucester Royal Hospital Special Baby
Unit and Gloucester AC Track Appeal Fund

GLOUCESTER A.C. 48 HOUR INTERNATIONAL TRACK RACE

Start 6p.m. 13/15th May 1983

COMPETITORS

* 1. MARTIN DAYKIN - GLOUCESTER AC   ENGLAND
      World No.2 100km 200 km 100 miles

* 2. DAVE DOWDLE - GLOUCESTER AC   ENGLAND
      World No.1 24 hrs.   No.3 100 mile

* 3. CHRIS O'CARROLL - GLOUCESTER AC   ENGLAND
      World top 25 24hr. track

* 4. KEN LEYSHON - GLOUCESTER AC   ENGLAND
      World ranked 24 hr. track

* 5. RICHARD DALBY - GLOUCESTER AC   ENGLAND
      World ranked top 20 50 mile track

* 6. JOHN JAMES - GLOUCESTER AC   ENGLAND
      Marathoneer

* 7. DAVE COOPER - CAMBRIDGE HARRIERS   ENGLAND
      Veteran ultra dist. runner
      World ranked 24 hrs.

* 8. KEN SHAW - CAMBRIDGE HARRIERS   ENGLAND
      Veteran ultra dist. runner

* 9. BOB HAMILTON - CHELTENHAM HARRIERS   ENGLAND
      Marathoneer/Newcomer

 10. MALCOLM CAMPBELL - NOTTS AC   ENGLAND
      Veteran world ranked ultra runner

 11. BRUCE SLADE - EXETER HARRIERS   ENGLAND
      World ranked ultra runner

*12. TERRY BURRIDGE - VERLEA AC   ENGLAND
      Experienced ultra dist. runner

 13. JOE TEASDALE - DURHAM CITY HARRIERS ENGLAND
      Experienced ultra dist. runner

 14. ROGER LAWTON - HOLMFIRTH HARRIERS   ENGLAND
      Experienced ultra dist. runner

 15. PAUL COLLINS - CANADA   CANADA
      Veteran ultra dist. runner

*16. RICHARD THORNTON - SALISBURY   ENGLAND
      Veteran ultra dist. runner

*17. COR VAN DER KOOY   HOLLAND
      Experienced ultra dist. runner

*18. FRED VAN BRUCHEM   HOLLAND
      Experienced ultra dist.runner

*19. HENK NOOR VEENWEG   HOLLAND
      Experienced ultra dist. runner

 20. RAY KROLEWICZ - PONTIAC   U.S.A.
      World ranked ultra dist. runner

 21. MARVIN SKAGERBERG - WEST SIDE YMCA   U.S.A.
      Veteran ultra dist.runner   NEW YORK

LADIES

*22. LYNN FITZGERALD - HIGHGATE HARRIERS ENGLAND
      World No.1 100 km. World No.2 24 hrs.

 23. ANN SAYER   ENGLAND
      World No.2 48 hr. track

4.   * 48 HOUR NEWCOMER   5.

PRESENTATION AWARDS

6.30 p.m. SUNDAY 15th MAY 1983

SPECIAL AWARDS

CITIZEN NEWSPAPER AWARD	First Gloucester Man
ERMINE PLANT HIRE	First Veteran
AFD SPAR (Calne)	Special Award

Certificates to all starters

Individual prize/award list

6.

Gloucester AC would like to record their thanks to the following for their much valued help and assistance:-

ANDY MILROY   R.R.C.

ERMINE PLANT HIRE LTD.

COMMITTEE GLOUCESTER ROYAL HOSPITAL
  BABY UNIT

ULTRAFAST SPORT/LEISURE

ST. JOHN AMBULANCE BRIGADE

MRS GRIFFITH   PYSIO
MRS O'CARROLL   MEDICAL

and all the officials and helpers both from within the Gloucester Club and from outside. Thank you also to those who donated trophies.

2.

167

OFFICIALS

Race Secretary	Chris O'Carroll
Race Liaison Officer	Terry Haines
Chief Timekeeper	Arthur Birt
Race Management by	Arthur and Shelagh Daley

MARSHALLS   GLOS AC
CATERERS   GLOS AC

3.

By now, Gloucester Athletics Club were getting pretty slick at organising these events! Don't know if you had noticed earlier in the book, but in the 100-mile, 24hr and 48hr races, we raised funds for various charities. This 48hr race was for Gloucester Royal Hospital's baby unit.

We also made people aware of our track appeal fund (from a cinder track to an all-weather track).

Extra special thanks to Ermin Plant Hire LTD, who again provided the floodlights for us and sent a team of men to set it all up! A lifesaver! It gave the track at night that intimate illumination that encouraged you to run, with a lovely atmosphere. One of the reasons it all came off okay.

I wrote a story about the race and the comments of the runners afterwards!

Start of 48hr race

ULTRA NEWS
48-HOUR TRACK RACE...
OUR LAST TOGETHER!

With the customary frantic last-minute details out of the way, the Gloucester AC 48-Hour Track Race finally got underway some 15 minutes late. The race was started by the Lord Mayor of Gloucester at 6.15 pm on Friday, 13th May, in cold, blustery conditions. Twenty-one runners made up the field, including one lady runner, Ann Sayer, from LWA. Also in the line-up were four ultra- distance runners from the home club, plus runners from France, USA and Holland, a mixture of seasoned ultra-distance men and some newcomers to this gruelling event.

At the 1-hour mark, a bunch of four runners, Daykin and Dalby from Glos AC, Burridge Verlea and Henk Noor Veenbeg, had covered 12.8km with the rest of the field close behind. Everything seemed to be ticking over nicely at this stage as the runners ran on into the gathering dust.

By the 4-hour mark, constant heavy rain showers and blustery winds were making conditions difficult, but the pattern remained the same with Glos AC now having three runners in the first four, Noor Veenbeg having dropped back.

The distances covered at this stage were:

Daykin 50.4km, Dalby 49.2km, Burridge 48.4km and Dowdle, the third Glos AC man, 47.2km. All four were well inside record schedule as was expected this early in the race.

Jean Pierre Haer, Paris, France (2nd. place) en route to two French records during Gloucester AC's 48 hour race 13/15th May, 1983.

By the 8-hour mark at 02:15hrs, the runners were well into the night and the weather had now calmed down. Daykin had covered 92.4km and was being tracked by club-mate Dowdle on 91.6km. Haer of France had moved into 3rd spot, covering 86.4km with Dalby now 4th but less than 1km behind the Frenchman. Things were looking good for Glos AC as the host club; perhaps Friday 13th was not a bad omen after all.

It was at this stage that fate intervened and Daykin suddenly pulled out of the race with no reason given and went home for a bath and a meal and some rest, with a view to rejoining the race later.

One hour later, he had not returned, but Dowdle had started to carve out a lead of 7km over Haer, with Dalby still in 3rd place. Non-stop walker Ann Sayer had moved up from 21st position with her huge stride pattern and was now lying in 14th place. By 04:15hrs, 2nd Glos runner, Dalby, was now in trouble, having covered only 3 miles in the previous hour.

With a quarter of the race gone, Dowdle was now some 6 miles ahead of Haer, with Dave Cooper, a vet from Cambridge Harriers, taking over 3rd place with Henk Noor Veenbeg up into 4th place. This time, Daykin had come back into 5th place in a valiant attempt to get going again but to no avail as both he and Dalby were in trouble now, and Paul Collins of Highgate Harriers had retired.

Dowdle reached the 100-mile mark in 14hrs 23mins 37secs, with Haer next in 15hrs 40mins 29secs, and these two were well clear of the vet, Cooper, in 3rd spot on 19hrs 13mins 14secs, with Ken Leyshon of Glos AC having worked his way up to 4th place on 20hrs 32mins 53secs.

At this point, Dowdle decided to take a break and slipped off home for 90mins to get a bath, a meal and watch some TV!

Once back on the track, he was looking fresh and was raring to go again, especially as Haer had taken the lead during his absence, the Frenchman having hardly rested at all. With no one else near them at this stage, these two were still on schedule for a record. Further down the field, much to the disappointment of spectators and officials alike, Ann Sayer had been forced to retire with both hips giving her trouble.

Whether or not it was the cinder track surface which forced her retirement, it was not known, but it was a great pity to see her go as she had shown great determination by forcing her way up to 13th position after being last earlier on.

At the 16hr stage, Haer was still leading Dowdle by 1km but like a Le Mans car, Dowdle had already made his refuelling stop, with the Frenchman yet to do so. Cooper was still hanging onto 3rd place, with Ken Leyshon in 4th. The leading four had covered at this stage 162.4km, 161.2km, 134km and 131.6km respectively.

After a gallant struggle, Dalby and Daykin were forced to retire, bringing the total of retirement to four at this stage, seventeen runners still remaining.

By the 20hr-mark, Haer was at last brought to a standstill, and during the course of his taking an hour's break, Dowdle went back to the front, taking a 6-mile lead during this time with Cooper still in 3rd spot.

By the halfway mark, the leading positions were as follows:

1st Dave Dowdle, UK, 136 miles approx, on schedule for world 48-hour best; 2nd Jean Haer, FR, 125 miles approx. Also within range of 48-hour best: 3rd Dave Cooper, UK, 121 miles; 4th Ken Leyshon, UK, 104miles; 5th Henk Noor Veenbeg, 103 miles; 6th Marvin Skagerberg, 101 miles.

It was ideal weather yet again on the second night with no wind and clear skies. The morale was sky high with a report between the runners and the lap recorders under the excellent supervision of Arthur Shelagh Daley as the race proceeded into the second half with all three main contenders running well.

The turning point of the race came after 28 hours had been completed, when Haer, who had earlier left the track for a 3- hour rest, fell into a deep sleep and had to be shaken by Glos AC race organiser, Chris O'Carroll. By this time, Dowdle, who had been running all the while that the Frenchman slept, had built up a massive lead, reaching the 250km mark 5 hours ahead of Haer. By this time, Cooper had moved into 2nd spot an hour ahead of Haer and the race was strictly between these three, although many private battles were going on down the field.

Skagerberg was slugging it out with Leyshon, and the evergreen Malcolm Campbell of Notts AC had run well to notch up 200km in 33hrs 55mins 03secs before he blew his chances of a good distance by leaving the track for 8 and a half hours' sleep.

Terry Burridge, who earlier had been going very well, was carrying one leg and making heavy weather of it, walking more than running but pluckily carrying on!

Gerard Stenger of France, currently world number 3, over 48 hours was suffering badly with sciatica, eventually being forced to retire.

Bruce Slade of Exeter was not having one of his better runs, although still in the top half of the field.

Two Dutch runners Cor van Der Kooy and Fred van Bruchen were both finding the going tough and had retired for the night. Fred, suffering with chest pains, decided to call it a day and promptly retired.

By the 32-hour mark, Dowdle had increased his lead, incredible running with only one big stop, but Haer had regained 2nd place with Cooper lying 3rd, Skagerberg 4th and Leyshon struggling along with a swollen ankle which reduced him to walking pace as he struggled in 5th position.

Dowdle was beginning to feel the strain as the race wore on, and by the 35th hour, he had slowed considerably. Apart from one longish break, he had run non-stop throughout. The news that revitalised Dave came from statistician Andy Milroy who informed him that the world best 300km figure was within reach. The current world record stood at 35hrs 28mins 15secs but the rejuvenated Dowdle raised his pace and, subject to ratification, passed the mark with 1min 12secs to spare.

Having achieved this peak, Dave began to suffer mentally and slowed once more and was again spurred on by the thought of beating the 200-mile record which stood at 38hrs 39mins 40secs.

Once more, he began to reel off lap after lap and took his second world record when he passed the 200-mile mark in 38hrs 34mins 16secs.

The problem now was how to keep him motivated and moving for a further 9 hours in an effort to crack the 48-hour record. The temptation to pack in with two records already to his credit must have been tremendous and indeed he left the track with this intention. Chris O'Carroll promptly gave him lots of food and drink, mainly tea, chocolate and natural honey, and coaxed him back onto the track to try a couple more laps to see how it went. With the encouragement, he got on his return, and he promptly reeled off another 29 laps, 7 and a quarter miles towards the 48-hour mark.

At the 40-hour stage, he was 30km ahead of Haer who in turn was 8km ahead of Cooper. The vet by this time was looking the stronger of the two and closing fast. Four hours later, Dowdle's lead was down to 23.2km with Cooper a further 13.6km behind Haer. Dowdle's gamble of taking little rest was beginning to pay off now as time ran out. Haer's 4-hour sleep had put the race out of his reach but he had the consolation of breaking the French 200-mile/300km records en route.

With two hours left, Dowdle was just going through the motions and circling the track like a zombie, still refusing to walk, and resting every few laps then running a few more. His distance at 46 hours was 370km or 231.25 miles so that on paper he had ample time to run the 11.6km required to equal the world best mark of 381.6km, the problem being that everyone watching had the feeling that if he stopped once, he would never start again. Haer and Cooper had long realised they had no chance of catching him and were solely intent on finishing in one piece.

With one hour left, Dave was running at an incredible pace. Still refusing to walk and looking in a terrible state, the wonder to everyone around the track was how he was managing to keep going at all.

Persuaded to leave the track for a change of clothing and some heavy liquid intake, as he was now suffering from dizziness as the sun began to shine, Dowdle was back on the track within 5 minutes and running incredibly again, and with the crowd urging him on, he went through the previous world best mark for 48 hours with 30 minutes to spare, his third world best mark in the race. This final effort proved to be the end for Dowdle, who managed just 2.45km before finishing completely exhausted after 48 hours. (238 miles+)

With two minutes to go, the rest of the field began to hurtle past Dowdle with miraculous last-minute recoveries, and so ended a memorable 48 hours for the Gloucester AC club!

So what at first seemed to be heading for a disaster with Daykin, Dalby, Collins, Bruchem and Ann Sayer, plus Gerard Stenger all out injured on the first day, who would have thought that so many records would fall on the second day with what remained on the field?

Dave Dowdle after a recovery period commented: "This was the hardest race mentally and physically that I have ever attempted and I am very proud to be the only man in history to hold the 24- and 48-hour world bests on the track at the same time. I cannot thank Chris O'Carroll enough both for organising the event and for helping me through the bad patches, especially after the 200-mile mark when I wanted to pack it in. To all the others who helped in any way, Arthur and Shelagh Daley, Arthur Birt, Andy Milroy and to my lap recorder who sat through the entire 48 hours, my thanks to all."

173

Dave Dowdle, Gloucester AC, going through the 48 hour world best mark during the 48 hour Track Race on 13/15th May, 1983, encouraged by organiser Chris O'Carroll.

Jean Haer echoed these sentiments when he said: "I'm grateful for having captured two French records, and if Chris O'Carroll hadn't woken me up, I wouldn't have had them."

Veteran Dave Cooper was "very pleased with my first attempt at 48hrs" and says: "I only wish I had come into ultra running earlier. My plan of running and then walking while taking my drinks and food worked out well for me, and I'd like to thank Gloucester AC for the fine organisation throughout, especially to all the lap recorders who worked so hard."

Looking down the results, Marvin Skagerberg was pleased with his 4th place, giving him a USA vets' record for the event. Gloucester's Ken Leyshon was pleased with his 5th place, although he didn't really run well by his standards and finished suffering with a badly swollen right leg.

So another Gloucester AC promotion came to a satisfactory conclusion. As it is the club's intention to put on another 100-mile road race next year, possibly in April, they may also include a 50km/ 100km race at the same time, they might well be billed as the unofficial 50/100km/100mile championships. I don't know of any other race especially over 50km on the road. Another Gloucester AC/UK first, perhaps.

Martin Daykin will probably be organising the 100-mile road race, and further news will be published when it is available.

Finally, to end on a light note, Ken Buckle of Cheltenham Harriers, who finished in 17th position in the 48hr, is said to be the only runner who ran/walked for 15 hours and slept for 33 hours! We think this must be some kind of a record. Ken definitely enjoyed himself and says he would do another and sometime soon.

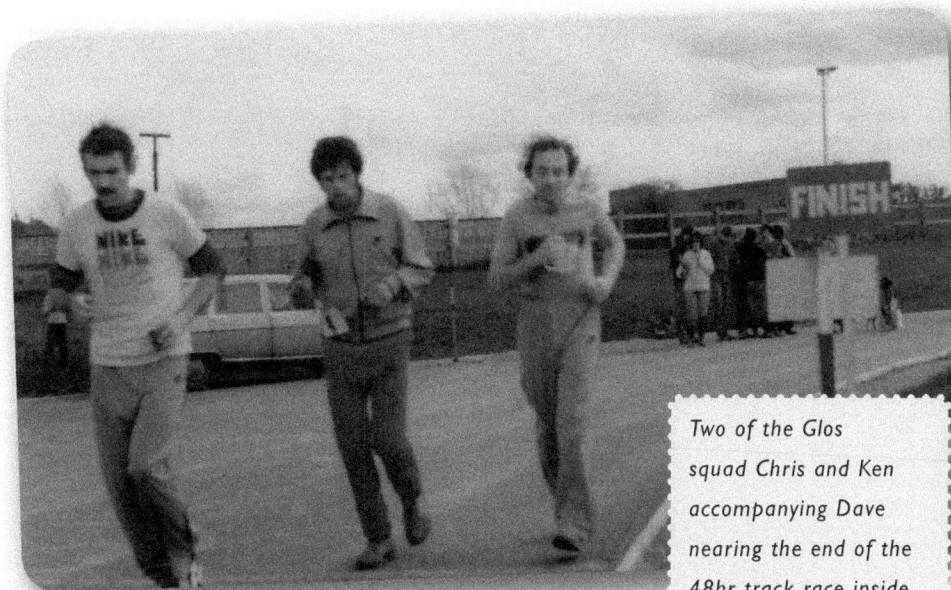

Two of the Glos squad Chris and Ken accompanying Dave nearing the end of the 48hr track race inside world record pace!

175

Dowdle is on top
of the world!

RECORDS
TUMBLE
TO DAVE

DIMINUTIVE Dave Dowdle has conquered the world again. Running in the Gloucester 48 hour race he broke three world records, adding to

Ken Leyshon with
Dave Dowdle

GLOUCESTER A.C. INVITATION 48 HOUR TRACK RACE

AT BLACKBRIDGE TRACT 6.00pm 13th MAY - 6.00pm 15th MAY 1983

			Metric Distance	Imperial Distance	
			km.	m.	yds.
1.	Dave Dowdle	Gloucester A.C.	384.050	238	1122
2.	Jean-Pierre Haec	France	368.370	228	1574
3.	Dave Cooper	Cambridge Harriers	351.888	218	1149
4.	Marvin Skagerberg	Westside YMCA U.S.A.	290.198	180	565
5.	Ken Leyshon	Gloucester A.C.	283.263	176	20
6.	Ken Shaw	Cambridge Harriers	269.410	167	720
7.	Henk Noor	Veenweg Holland	257.979	160	529
8.	Malcolm Campbell	Notts A.C.	239.600	148	1550
9.	Bruce Slade	Exeter Harriers	239.200	148	112
10.	Terry Burbridge	Verlea A.C.	235.139	146	192
11.	Roger Lawton	Holmfirth Harriers	221.947	137	1604
12.	Cor Van Der Kooy	Holland	216.324	134	735
13.	Richard Thornton	Salisbury	187.915	122	1723
14.	Jacques de Roquefeuil	France	183.643	114	195
15.	Gerard Stenger	France	136.000	84	891
16.	Fred Van Bruchem	Holland	125.600	78	78
17.	Ken Buckle	Cheltenham & C Harriers	116.00	72	139
18.	Richard Dalby	Gloucester A.C.	110.400	68	1055
19.	Martin Daykin	Gloucester A.C.	109.600	68	180
=20.	Paul Collins	Canada	100.00	62	241
=20	Ann Sayer	England	100.000	62	241

PERFORMANCES SUBMITTED FOR RATIFICATION

DAVE DOWDLE
1 48 hr. track running 384.050   World best performance
2 300km. 35 hrs 27 mins 03 secs   "   "   "
3 200 miles 38 hrs 34 mins 16 secs   "   "   "

JEAN PIERRE HAEC
4 200 miles 42 hrs 57 mins 09 secs   FRENCH RECORD
5 300 km. 40 hrs 19 mins 07 secs   "

DAVE COOPER
6 48HR 351.888   WORLD BEST VET
7 300 km. 41 hrs 31 mins 01 secs   WORLD BEST VETS
8 200 miles 44 hrs 24 mins 08 secs   "

9 MARVIN SKAGERBERG 290 km 180 MILES   USA RECORD VETS

HENK NOOR   ~~V80MLS~~ ~~XXXX48HR~~ ——— HOLLAND REC
10 24 HRS 101.5 MLS   — " —
11 48 HRS 160.529 MLS   — " —

177

	1 hour		2 hours		3 hours		4 hours	
Dowdle	12.4	5	24.4	5	36.0	4	47.2	4
Haec	12.4	5	24.4	5	36.0	4	46.8	5
Cooper	11.6	7	22.4	7	33.6	7	44.0	7
Skagerberg	11.2	10	21.2	13	31.2	13	40.0	11
Leyshon	11.2	10	22.0	9	32.0	8	39.2	13
Shaw	10.8	19	20.8	17	30.0	15	39.2	13
Noor	12.8	1	25.6	1	35.6	6	45.2	6
Campbell	10.8	19	20.4	18	28.8	18	36.8	18
Slade	11.6	7	22.4	7	32.0	8	40.8	9
Burbridge	12.8	1	24.8	4	37.2	3	48.4	3
Lawton	11.2	10	21.2	13	30.0	15	40.0	11
Kooy	10.4	20	20.0	19	28.8	18	36.4	19
Thornton	10.8	19	20.0	19	28.0	20	34.8	20
Roquefeuil	11.2	10	21.2	13	31.2	13	40.4	10
Stenger	11.2	10	21.6	11	32.0	8	42.0	8
Bruchem	11.6	7	22.0	9	31.6	12	38.0	15
Buckle	11.2	10	21.6	11	32.0	8	37.6	17
Dalby	12.8	1	25.6	1	38.4	1	49.2	2
Daykin	12.8	1	25.6	1	38.0	2	50.4	1
Cullins	10.8	19	21.2	13	30.0	15	38.0	15
Sayer	8.0	21	16.0	21	23.6	21	31.2	21

5 hours		6 hours		7 hours		8 hours		9 hours	
57.6	3	68.8	3	80.4	2	91.6	2	103.6	1
56.4	5	66.4	5	75.6	3	86.4	3	96.4	2
53.2	7	62.8	6	72.0	6	81.6	6	86.4	7
48.0	9	55.6	10	63.2	9	71.6	8	78.8	9
47.2	13	54.8	12	62.0	11	69.2	11	79.2	8
48.0	9	56.0	8	63.6	8	71.6	8	78.4	10
55.2	6	62.8	6	71.6	7	80.0	7	88.4	6
43.2	18	47.2	19	53.6	18	61.2	16	69.6	17
47.6	12	50.8	15	60.0	13	70.4	10	72.8	11
57.6	3	66.8	4	73.6	5	82.8	5	90.8	5
46.4	14	54.0	14	61.6	12	61.6	15	61.6	16
42.0	20	50.0	16	55.2	16	62.4	14	68.8	13
42.4	19	48.8	17	55.2	16	63.2	13	63.2	15
48.0	9	54.8	12	58.4	15	58.4	19	58.4	19
50.4	8	59.2	8	59.2	14	60.8	17	60.8	18
44.8	16	48.0	18	48.4	20	49.6	20	57.6	20
44.0	17	44.0	20	44.0	21	44.0	21	44.0	21
59.6	2	70.0	2	75.6	3	85.6	4	92.8	3
62.8	1	75.2	1	85.2	1	92.4	1	92.4	4
46.0	15	55.2	11	63.2	9	70.0	11	70.0	12
38.0	21	45.6	21	52.8	19	60.0	18	67.6	14

	10 hrs		11 hrs		12 hrs		13 hrs		14 hrs	
Dowdle	114.4	1	124.4	1	135.2	1	145.6	1	156.0	1
Haec	106.0	:2	117.2	2	125.6	2	136.4	2	147.2	2
Cooper	94.8	6	103.2	4	112.8	3	120.8	3	127.6	3
Skagerberg	87.6	8	95.2	7	102.8	7	108.8	7	118.4	4
Leyshon	87.6	8	94.8	8	102.4	9	102.4	.9	113.2	6
Shaw	78.4	11	85.2	11	92.8	11	99.6	11	106.4	11
Noor	96.0	5	98.4	6	106.8	4	112.0	4	112.0	7
Campbell	76.0	18	83.2	12	88.0	14	96.0	13	102.8	12
Slade	81.2	10	88.4	10	95.2	10	101.6	10	108.0	9
Burbridge	98.0	4	103.2	4	103.6	6	110.8	5	116.8	5
Lawton	63.2	16	72.0	15	72.0	16	86.8	15	93.2	15
Kooy	76.0	12	83.2	12	89.2	12	93.4	14	100.4	13
Thornton	63.2	16	63.2	18	67.6	18	75.2	12	81.2	18
Roquefeuil	58.4	20	58.4	20	58.4	20	58.4	20	59.2	20
Stenger	60.8	19	60.8	19	60.8	19	60.8	19	60.8	19
Bruchem	64.0	15	70.0	16	77.2	15	80.0	16	83.2	16
Buckle	44.0	21	44.0	21	44.0	21	44.0	21	53.6	21
Dalby	101.6	3	104.4	3	104.4	5	106.4	8	108.0	9
Daykin	92.4	7	92.4	9	102.8	7	109.6	8	109.6	8
Cullins	70.0	14	70.0	16	70.0	17	75.2	17	82.4	17
Sayer	74.8	13	82.4	14	89.2	12	96.4	12	100.0	14

15 hrs		16 hrs		17 hrs		18 hrs		19 hrs	
156.0	1	161.2	2	171.2	1	180.8	1	188.4	1
154.0	2	162.4	1	171.2	1	176.0	2	184.8	2
127.6	3	134.0	3	140.0	3	149.2	3	158.0	3
118.4	4	118.8	7	120.0	7	130.0	7	136.8	6
123.2	4	131.6	4	135.2	4	144.0	4	146.0	4
112.8	8	118.0	8	118.0	8	126.8	8	126.8	8
118.4	6	124.4	6	129.2	6	133.2	6	133.6	6
102.8	13	108.8	11	115.6	9	122.8	10	126.0	11
108.0	10	115.2	9	115.2	10	124.4	9	128.4	7
122.8	5	127.6	5	133.2	5	135.2	5	139.2	5
100.0	14	106.0	14	111.2	12	118.8	11	121.2	11
104.8	12	107.6	13	115.2	10	117.6	12	122.0	10
84.4	17	91.2	17	91.2	18	97.6	16	100.0	13
70.0	19	76.8	19	86.8	19	90.4	17	90.4	17
60.8	20	66.4	21	76.8	20	87.2	18	97.6	16
83.2	18	90.4	18	96.4	17	101.2	14	106.0	12
53.6	21	68.0	20	76.0	21	77.2	19	84.	18
108.0	10	108.0	12	108.0	14	110.4	13		
109.6	9	109.6	10	109.6	13				
91.6	16	97.6	16	97.6	16	100.0	15	100.0	13

	20 hrs		21 hrs		22 hrs		23 hrs		24 hrs
Dowdle	197.2	1	206.0	1	209.6	1	210.0	1	219.2
Haec	184.8	2	190.8	2	199.6	2	206.0	2	206.8
Cooper	162.4	3	170.8	3	178.8	3	187.6	3	196.0
Skagerberg	145.6	5	153.6	5	159.6	5	165.2	4	168.0
Leyshon	155.6	4	160.0	4	160.0	4	160.6	6	160.0
Shaw	135.6	9	140.4	9	146.4	9	152.0	10	158.4
Noor	138.4	7	150.0	6	150.0	8	155.2	7	162.4
Campbell	132.8	10	139.2	10	146.4	9	152.8	9	161.2
Slade	136.8	8	143.6	8	152.4	7	154.4	8	163.2
Burbridge	145.2	6	149.6	7	155.6	6	160.8	5	160.8
Lawton	128.0	11	135.2	11	142.0	11	146.8	11	155.6
Kooy	128.0	11	129.2	12	129.2	12	134.0	12	137.6
Thornton	105.6	16	111.2	15	114.0	14	114.4	15	121.2
Roquefeuil	90.4	17	95.2	16	95.6	17	95.6	17	95.6
Stenger	104.4	17	111.6	14	111.6	15	116.4	14	125.2
Bruchem	110.4	13	113.2	13	116.4	13	120.0	13	125.6
Buckle	90.0	18	92.4	17	102.0	16	102.0	16	104.4

	25 hrs		26 hrs		27 hrs		28 hrs	
1	226.4	1	233.6	1	241.6	1	249.6	1
2	214.4	2	221.6	2	228.0	2	230.4	2
3	196.0	3	200.0	3	208.4	3	216.8	3
4	168.0	4	170.8	5	179.2	4	187.2	4
9	167.6	5	174.4	4	177.6	5	184.0	5
10	162.8	8	165.6	8	170.8	8	176.8	7
6	166.0	6	170.6	0	170.0	9	170.0	9
7	161.2	9	165.2	9	172.8	7	174.8	8
5	163.6	7	168.8	7	175.6	6	177.2	6
8	160.8	10	160.8	11	160.8	11	160.8	11
11	155.6	11	161.2	10	161.2	10	166.4	10
12	142.4	12	146.0	12	146.0	12	146.0	12
15	122.8	13	128.0	14	133.2	14	133.2	14
17	95.6	16	95.6	16	102.4	15	102.4	15
14	125.2	14	134.8	13	134.8	13	136.0	13
13	111.2	15	116.0	15				

	29 hrs		30 hrs		31 hrs		32 hrs		33 hrs
Dowdle	254.8	1	258.4	1	266.4	1	272.0	1	279.2
Haec	238.0	2	244.0	2	244.0	2	244.0	2	244.0
Cooper	221.2	3	228.0	3	228.0	3	233.6	3	241.6
Skagerberg	193.2	4	200.0	4	205.6	4	208.0	4	212.8
Leyshon	187.2	5	189.2	5	193.6	5	198.4	5	199.6
Shaw	183.6	6	185.6	6	189.6	6	194.0	6	194.0
Noor	170.0	10	175.2	10	185.6	7	190.0	7	190.0
Campbell	174.8	8	177.2	9	184.0	9	190.0	7	194.8
Slade	180.0	7	185.2	7	185.2	8	188.8	9	193.2
Burbridge	160.8	11	160.8	11	166.0	11	170.8	11	175.2
Lawton	172.0	9	179.2	8	179.2	10	179.2	10	180.0
Kooy	146.0	12	150.0	12	155.6	12	160.4	12	162.0
Thornton	133.2	14	133.2	14	133.2	14	133.2	14	137.6
Roquefeuil	102.4	15	102.4	15	102.4	15	102.4	15	102.4

	34 hrs		35 hrs		36 hrs		37 hrs		38 hrs	
1	287.2	1	295.6	1	302.4	1	310.0	1	316.0	1
2	244.0	3	249.2	3	258.0	3	267.6	2	276.8	2
3	248.8	2	256.4	2	261.6	2	264.4	3	272.0	3
4	218.4	4	218.4	4	220.4	4	222.4	4	222.4	4
5	202.0	5	202.0	6	206.8	6	213.2	5	220.4	5
7	200.8	6	206.4	5	210.4	5	210.8	6	218.4	6
9	190.0	9	190.0	9	194.8	8	202.4	7	207.6	7
6	200.0	7	200.0	7	200.0	7	200.0	8	200.0	8
8	193.2	8	193.2	8	193.2	9	193.2	10	193.2	11
11	181.2	10	185.2	10	190.0	10	194.8	9	200.0	8
10	180.0	11	180.0	11	180.0	11	188.4	11	196.4	10
12	162.0	12	162.0	12	1620.	12	166.4	12	171.6	12
13	143.6	13	145.2	13	145.2	13	145.2	13	145.2	13
15	102.4	15	102.4	15	102.4	15	105.2	14	115.6	14

	39 hrs		40 hrs		41 hrs		42 hrs		43 hrs	
Dowdle	322.4	1	326.4	1	332.4	1	338.8	1	346.8	1
Haec	286.0	2	296.4	2	304.4	2	314.0	2	322.0	2
Cooper	280.0	3	288.4	3	295.2	3	302.4	3	309.2	3
Skagerberg	225.6	5	233.6	5	242.0	4	248.0	4	254.8	4
Leyshon	227.2	4	235.2	4	241.6	5	247.2	5	250.8	5
Shaw	223.6	6	229.2	6	235.6	6	240.8	6	242.4	6
Noor	212.0	7	216.8	7	222.8	7	228.4	7	233.2	7
Campbell	200.0	8	200.0	10	202.4	10	208.0	10	215.6	8
Slade	193.2	11	193.2	11	195.6	11	201.2	11	208.8	11
Burbridge	200.0	8	204.4	8	207.6	8	208.4	9	210.4	9
Lawton	196.4	10	203.6	9	207.6	8	209.2	8	209.2	10
Kooy	178.0	12	180.4	12	186.4	12	191.2	12	192.8	12
Thornton	156.0	13	161.2	13	161.6	13	167.2	13	173.6	13
Roquefeuil	124.8	14	129.2	14	134.0	14	136.0	14	142.8	14

44 hrs		45 hrs		46 hrs		47 hrs		48 hrs	
354.8	1	362.4	1	370.0	1	377.2	1	384.050	1
331.6	2	339.2	2	348.8	2	358.0	2	368.370	2
318.0	3	325.6	3	333.6	3	341.2	3	351.888	3
262.0	4	268.4	4	275.2	4	282.8	4	290.198	4
257.6	5	261.6	5	268.8	5	275.2	5	283.663	5
247.6	6	251.6	6	256.4	6	262.8	6	269.469	6
238.4	7	243.2	7	247.6	7	252.0	7	257.979	7
217.2	8	224.4	8	229.6	8	232.4	8	239.600	8
210.4	10	217.6	10	223.2	10	232.4	9	239.200	9
212.0	9	218.4	9	224.0	9	228.4	10	235.140	10
209.2	11	209.2	11	210.4	11	215.6	11	221.947	11
198.0	12	200.4	12	205.6	12	210.0	12	216.324	12
176.4	13	182.8	13	186.0	13	192.0	13	197.915	13
152.8	14	157.2	14	163.6	14	173.2	14	183.643	14

! DAVE DOWDLE WORLD RECORD !

384.05 KM / 48 HRS

FOR YOU STATISTIC ANALYSISTS

Statistics of Dave Dowdles 10km splits on his way to world record 48hrs including rest of competitors also for you appraisal.

	10 km	20 km	30 km	40 km	50 km
D.Dowdle	48.36	1.38.08	2.28.37	3.21.47	4.17.0
J.P.Haec	48.38	1.38.48	2.30.15	3.23.20	4.19.59
D.Cooper	53.05	1.46.05	2.42.10	3.38.08	4.37.17
M.Skagerberg	54.07	1.52.00	2.53.22	4.01.15	5.13.43
K.Leyshon	53.12	1.46.32	2.52.52	4.04.48	5.13.45
K.Shaw	56.10	1.57.00	3.01.20	4.05.46	5.12.44
Henk Noor	47.43	1.34.33	2.33.38	3.24.41	4.32.22
M.Campbell	54.05	1.57.51	3.12.08	4.31.24	6.22.10
B.Slade	51.55	1.48.26	2.48.22	3.57.08	5.53.30
T.Burbridge	47.44	1.35.17	2.26.46	3.16.17	4.09.31
R.Lawton	53.35	1.52.58	3.02.05	3.59.40	5.26.53
Cor van der Kooy	58.18	2.02.00	3.10.11	4.33.42	5.58.45
R.Thornton	56.18	2.02.07	3.14.02	4.37.09	6.18.05
J.Roquefeuil	54.38	1.53.04	2.54.42	3.59.20	5.15.40
F.Van Bruchem	51.23	1.50.08	2.51.04	4.16.08	8.02.21
G.Stenger	53.26	1.49.58	2.48.22	3.49.40	4.56.14
K.Buckle	55.22	1.51.56	2,46.22	4.20.17	13.38.53
R.Dalby	46.46	1.33.54	2.21.00	3.09.54	4.05.52
M.Daykin	47.00	1.32.34	2.22.21	3.09.57	3.58.10
P.Collins	54.43	1.52.23	3.02.44	4.19.20	5.25.49
Ann Sayer	1.16.55	2.34.10	3.52.57	5.13.10	6.38.25

	60 km	70 km	80 km	90 km	100 km	110 km
	5.11.01	6.04.52	6.57.40	7.49.55	8.42.08	9.35.28
	5.20.30	6.25.38	7.22.15	8.22.49	9.21.20	10.21.21
	5.42.12	6.44.36	7.48.22	9.28.18	10.39.48	11.46.18
	6.34.34	7.45.27	9.08.37	10.19.33	11.38.24	13.07.00
	6.40.40	8.12.18	9.07.20	10.13.24	11.34.43	13.41.10
	6.32.25	7.48.36	9.10.16	11.35.00	13.08.23	14.37.28
	5.24.52	6.45.40	8.07.30	9.10.51	11.11.19	12.29.47
	7.46.35	9.03.50	10.34.35	12.13.44	13.33.16	16.18.24
	6.58.15	7.57.52	9.51.31	11.29.19	12.50.58	14.22.33
	5.14.05	6.23.54	7.40.23	8.54.53	10.13.32	12.50.33
	6.34.38	10.46.43	11.48.46	13.25.44	14.44.40	16.50.28
	7.33.00	9.08.02	10.36.54	12.06.28	13.47.24	16.28.02
	7.34.16	12.21.28	13.44.18	15.50.18	18.18.23	20.50.47
	14.03.38	14.59.41	16.18.16	17.50.19	26.38.46	37.26.12
	9.29.46	10.46.49	12.24.28	15.52.06	17.34.52	19.54.36
	6.04.20	16.19.34	17.17.15	18.16.08	19.31.26	20.41.58
	14.38.00	16.14.52	18.35.25	19.48.35		
	5.00.15	5.59.22	7.24.18	8.38.44	9.43.42	
	4.46.30	5.34.12	6.23.35	7.22.34	11.43.53	
	6.34.28	7.47.24	13.27.18	14.47.29	16.21.45	
	7.57.57	9.19.48	10.42.33	12.05.24	13.29.51	

	120 km	130 km	140 km	150 km	160 km
D.Dowdle	10.30.13	11.29.59	12.26.00	13.25.21	14.23.37
J.P.Haec	11.26.15	12.22.28	13.17.37	14.16.36	15.40.29
D.Cooper	12.53.58	15.33.37	16.57.08	18.04.32	19.13.14
M.Skagerberg	16.58.13	17.56.25	19.19.15	20.32.46	22.00.46
K.Leyshon	14.40.26	15.35.45	17.32.13	19.22.30	20.32.53
K.Shaw	16.16.27	18.39.58	20.53.37	22.35.57	24.14.18
Henk Noor	15.12.24	17.06.06	20.19.15	21.28.32	23.33.30
M.Campbell	17.40.00	19.33.05	21.05.12	22.26.17	23.53.24
B.Slade	17.28.44	19.09.36	20.42.07	21.43.40	23.39.03
T.Burbridge	14.27.02	16.21.36	19.09.21	21.01.16	22.44.50
R.Lawton	18.06.27	20.17.20	21.46.17	23.21.33	25.40.00
Cor van der Kooy	18.45.04	22.29.20	24.21.10	29.54.32	31.54.39
R.Thornton	23.45.10	26.16.05	33.21.21	38.04.04	39.44.32
J.Roquefeuil	38.27.38	40.05.42	42.33.30	43.43.55	45.15.40
F.Van Bruchem	22.54.35				
G.Stenger	23.24.32	24.31.38			

170km	180km	190km	200km	210km	220km
16.52.32	17.55.12	19.07.16	20.16.24	22.59.11	24.06.31
16.52.57	18.31.38	20.52.44	22.03.36	24.21.08	25.44.32
20.51.47	22.05.54	23.15.12	25.57.39	27.10.18	28.43.16
25.53.30	27.03.49	28.30.56	29.56.18	32.34.28	35.50.35
25.29.11	27.19.36	30.27.13	33.00.49	36.25.55	37.48.52
26.46.55	28.30.48	31.01.28	33.53.25	35.52.36	38.15.22
25.33.40	30.26.34	31.59.37	36.37.49	38.41.24	40.30.34
26.31.58	30.23.50	31.55.50	33.53.03	42.11.57	44.25.51
26.12.12.	28.58.43	32.15.02	41.32.44	43.08.43	45.14.14
31.51.27	33.46.07	35.58.58	37.56.23	42.20.56	45.18.16
28.28.26	30.04.17	37.12.19	39.30.36	45.53.47	47.48.24
37.29.49	39.53.59	41.44.48	44.13.18	46.57.57	
42.24.39	44.32.19	46.39.48			
46.38.25	47.42.16				

	230 km	240 km	250 km	260 km	270 km
D.Dowdle	25.37.42	26.48.41	28.01.49	30.09.40	31.44.01
J.P.Haec	27.54.59	29.25.05	35.04.11	36.10.21	37.14.25
D.Cooper	31.32.40	32.46.54	34.06.47	35.27.00	37.44.56
M.Skagerberg	39.33.03	40.44.39	42.11.33	43.42.09	45.10.25
K.Leyshon	39.19.04	40.39.22	42.24.33	44.30.07	46.06.57
K.Shaw	40.04.35	41.49.55	44.27.52	46.29.56	
Henk Noor	43.42.09	45.10.25	46.29.37		
M.Campbell	46.00.32				
B.Slade	46.36.19				
T.Burbridge	47.12.54				

280 km	290 km	300 km	310 km	320 km	330 km
33.04.55	34.16.58	35.27.03	36.56.22	38.23.40	40.39.39
38.23.55	39.20.48	40.19.07	41.33.10	42.46.25	43.46.22
38.55.32	40.22.02	31.31.01	43.02.50	44.10.54	45.27.58
46.37.26	47.59.09				
47.46.05					

	340 km	350 km	360 km	370 km	380 km
D.Dowdle	42.08.40	43.23.16	44.40.16	45.56.45	47.18.25
J.P.Haec	45.03.40	46.07.13	47.11.27		
D.Cooper	46.49.39	47.50.25			

Chris O'Carroll
alongside Dave Dowdle.

SUMMARY OF OUR GLOUCESTER AC
48HR TRACK RACE

Five world bests! Two French records! Three Dutch records! One USA record! Plus a few personal records also!

On hindsight, Dave Dowdle was proved right not to complete the 24-hour relay race previously, (with the horrendous weather).

Martin Daykin suffered earlier on in the 48-hour race and retired early on.

Ken Leyshon had a badly swollen leg but still managed to finish with a creditable 176miles+!

So another successful event completed. I honestly think (apart from the London area), the Gloucester City Athletic Track has more World, European and British records than any other athletics tracks in Britain for ultra-distance running, but I may be wrong!

I can't thank enough all of the people who helped to put the whole show on the road, with terrific team work and organisation!

THE FINALE!

Well that's it!

Our last race together

I hope you enjoyed reading the book! Never would imagine the story that unfolded! It seems like a whirlwind of organisation, training, travelling and racing! Lots of hints, tips and lessons that might be of use to yourself on your own journey throughout your running life. As you can gather from reading the book, running is about having a go and achieving the impossible. We had great help along the way from family, friends and athletic club members! Sometimes total strangers helped us along our way when staging some of our races in the UK!

Special mention to our gallant lap recorders who sat through rain, wind and snow. (No chips in them days.)

Also, acknowledgements to the following clubs for their valuable support throughout:

- Gloucester Athletic Club
- Cheltenham Harriers AC
- Bourton Road Runners
- Leamington Spa C&AC
- Tipton Harriers AC

Most of the overseas entrants and their supporters really enjoyed their stay here in Gloucester and said they would always remember the events that we put on.

The two lady pioneers who ran in our 24-hour track race will always remember the support they got from everybody who was there at the race!

We will also remember the organisation and cock-ups when racing abroad… we all laugh about it and always will.

We were all pioneers in our day in the early 1980s! But look now, thousands of you runners are now running in 50k and 100k+ (mainly trail races) distances.

I think when you are younger, you tend to see how fast you can run, but as you get older, more and more runners see how far they can run!

Everyone has completed a 10k and 1/2 marathon, then onto a marathon. A lot stop at the marathon. "Never again," (I said that) but quite a lot of you suddenly think, I wonder if I can go further.

To cut a long story short, I entered a 100km trail race in 2016 called 'Race to the Stones'. When I got there, thousands were already there, both men and ladies. The hooter started and away they went, running and walking up to 50km or on up to 100km!

All enjoying it in their own way! I always say that when you have done an ultra-distance race, the experience and the absolute joy you feel when you sink into a big hot bath with a lovely mug of tea or coffee, or a pint of beer after a hard day's running… it's sheer bliss; there is nothing in this life quite like it!

ACKNOWLEDGEMENTS

A few special mentions need to go firstly to Liz Daykin, for the preparation and making of this book, which without her help would never have happened! To Arthur Daley and his team of helpers specifically for keeping the whole show running smoothly for the 24 & 48hr track races, enabling me to run my own race. And to fellow teammates Martin Daykin, Ken Leyshon and Dave Dowdle, who were all part of this amazing running journey we went on. Lastly to my wife and family, who were never far away from all these events, on a bike, with a cup of water or a sponge!

This book is also dedicated to the memory of Cavin Woodward of Leamington AC, Don Richie of Aberdeen AAC, Martin Daykin of Gloucester AC, Andy Holden of Tipton Harriers, Ron Bently of Tipton Harriers.

Five Ultra Road Running Legends never forgotten.

ABOUT THE AUTHOR
BY HIS DAUGHTERS, CHRISTINA, CATHERINE & CLAIRE O'CARROLL

Our dad has carried on competing well into his seventies; going back to his first love of athletics, in both track and field events. He is currently a Gloucester County Champion in various field and track events for his ever-changing age groups: Long Jump, Hammer, Shot, 100m, 200m, up to 1500m where he often gets acknowledged by the younger generations! Dad did a 24hr track ultra-distance race in 2017 on the same world record track; however, after 12 hours, an injured foot stopped him going for the 24 hours.

He always encourages people to have a go at anything in their lives and to enjoy it, whatever sport it is. He is an inspiration and has endless energy with a diary of daily activities logged for the past 7 or 8 years proving that when you can see what you've achieved, it helps push you to keep going.

Heart and sole

FOREST runner Chris O'Carroll took on a gruelling 100-kilometre race to raise funds for a life-saving machine.

Chris decided to raise money for a portable heart defibrillator which would be available for track and cross-country events around Gloucestershire after a running friend died after finishing a race.

The 72-year-old from Broadwell took part in the Race to the Stones which finishes at the prehistoric stone circle at Avebury in Wiltshire.

Chris, who set world records in the 1980s with the Gloucestershire ultra-distance squad, finished in a time of 20 hours and 47 minutes and was first in his age category.

He said: "After seeing runners die I thought I would raise funds to buy a portable heart defibrillator which would be available for use at any track or cross-country event in Gloucestershire.

"More and more people are taking up running and there has been an increase in sudden heart deaths among younger people in all sports.

"A defibrillator could be the difference between life and death so if we could get one which would be available to organisers of events that would be an enormous step forward."

Donations can be made online at www.crowdfunding.justgiving.com/chrisgloucesterac.

Cheques can be sent to Gloucester Athletic Track Management, 13 Ardmore Close, Tuffley, Gloucester, GL4 0BJ.

•*Chris O'Carroll with his medal from the Race to the Stones.*

24hr race after 12hrs

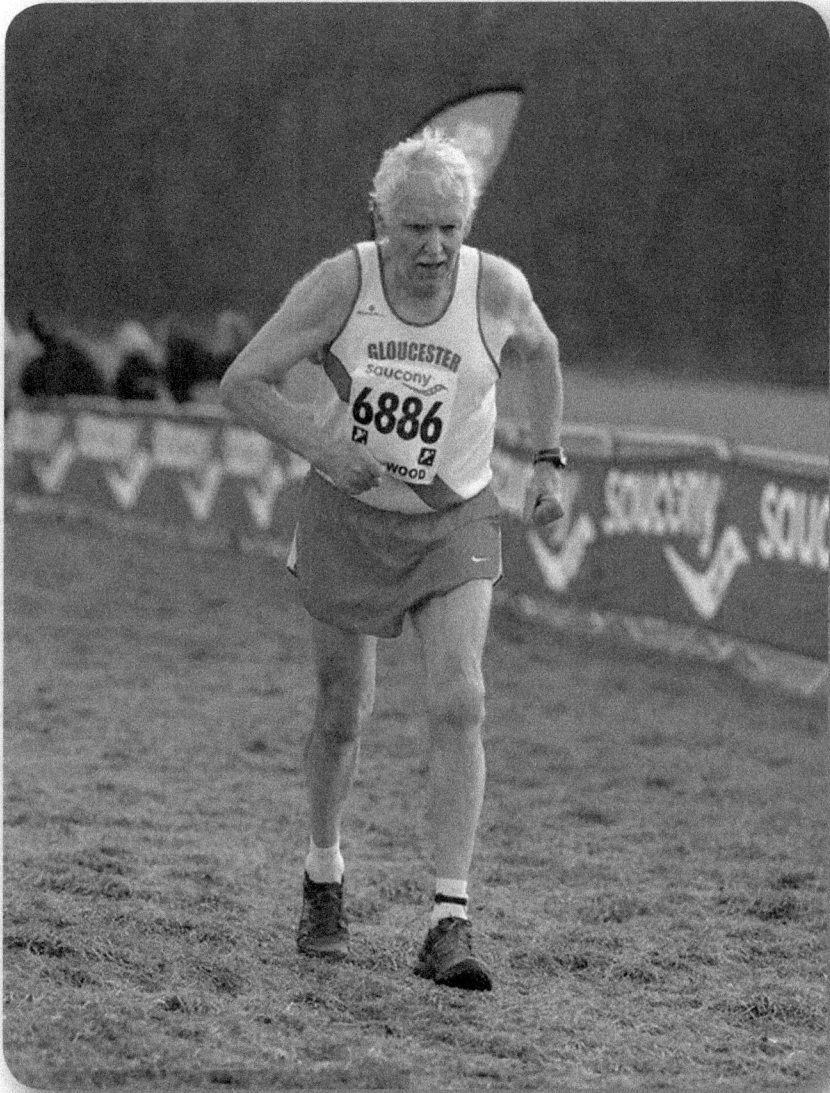

Cross country league
still competing

*Just before 5am finishing
Race to the Stones
100km aged 74*

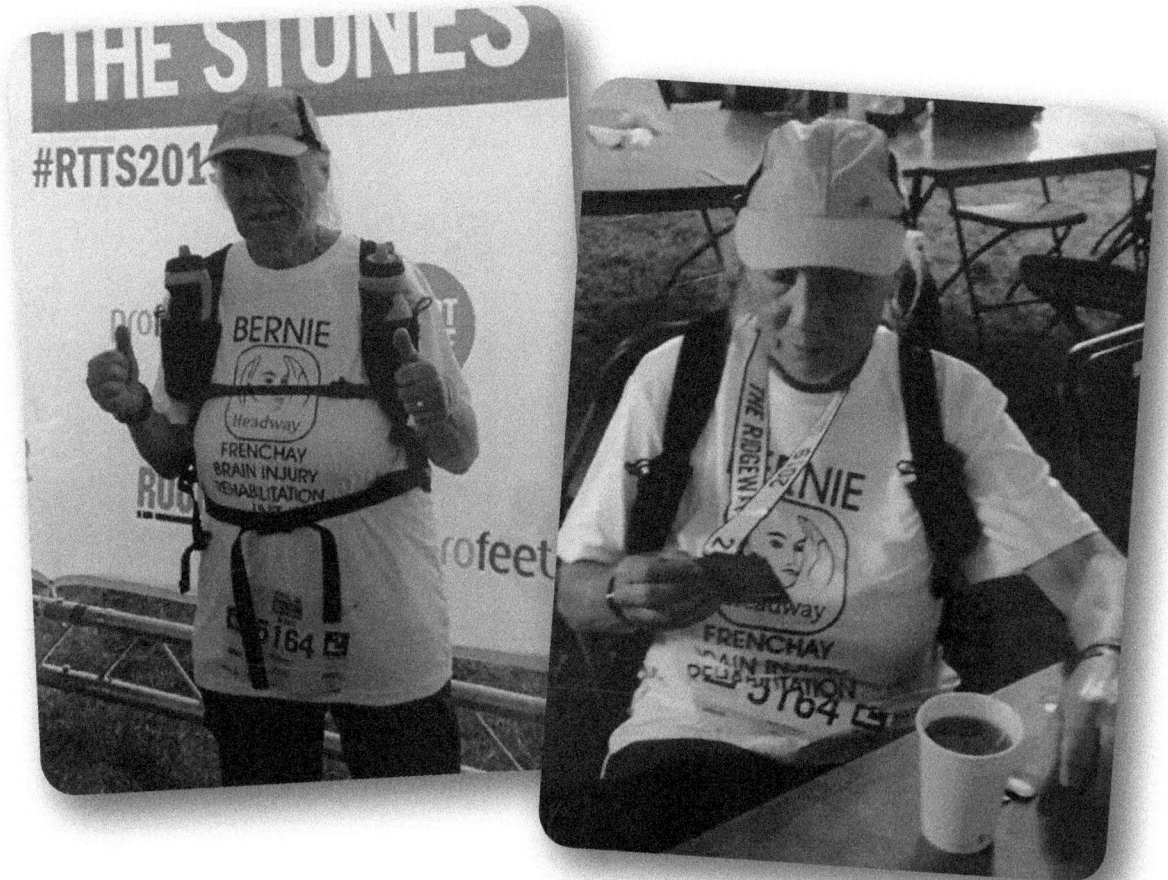

After years supporting our dad and all his races, our mum Bernie decided to do the 50km Race to The Stones at age 68 and enjoyed it so much she decided to do it again in 2019 aged 70 finishing with a celebratory cup of tea!

If you can't beat them, join them!

This poem came to me on a crisp, sunny Sunday morning while running in Cranham Woods, with the distant bells of the church in Painswick Glos ringing faintly in the distance!

A Runner's Glimpse of Heaven

Quietly stepping out the door
Off for a run twenty miles or more
Up the road off into the woods
Spirits soaring, never knew life would be so good!
Legs and heart do gently pound
Running along with hardly a sound
Except for frosty leaves crunched underfoot
onto the ground.

Rabbits startled bolt down their holes
Running on through fields with mounds dug up by moles
Spiders' webs glisten with dew in the morning sun
Craftily awaiting the first insects to fly in trapped upon!
A jay shrieks out its startled cry
As badger and fox creep stealthily by.

On and on leaping over stile gate and brook
Kingfisher flashes by with fish just took
Running over the hills and down the dells
Faintly in the distance Harken! Church bells!
Crow and Rook argue high in trees above
as alas the last gate is opened with a gentle shove!

Running back down onto the road
As if leaving a dream and beauty
Of wonder and peaceful sanity
Back down the road, back into reality
Into the house and through the door
Sweaty running kit strewn about the floor
Come sun, rain, hail, sleet or snow
I'll be back up the road
Into the woods again tomorrow!

By Chris O'Carroll

Matador

For exclusive discounts on Matador titles,
sign up to our occasional newsletter at
troubador.co.uk/bookshop